D0772591

Jazz Modernism

OVERLEAF: 1. Pablo Picasso, *Figure for a Monument to Guillaume Apollinaire*, 1928. Metal cable construction. 45¼" high. One of four wire maquettes executed that year by Julio González to Picasso's specifications. The project was never realized. In 1962 a twelve-foot-high steel version was cast for Picasso, who donated it to the Museum of Modern Art in 1972.

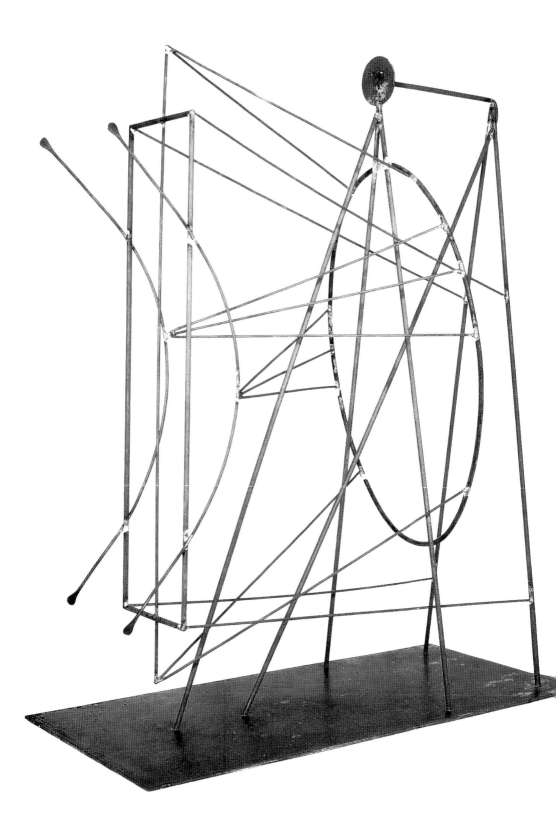

Jazz
Modernism

from
Ellington
and
Armstrong
to
Matisse
and
Joyce

Alfred Appel, Jr.

 Alfred A. Knopf New York 2002

This Is a Borzoi Book Published by Alfred A. Knopf

Copyright © 2002 by Alfred Appel, Jr.

Published in the United States by Alfred A. Knopf, a division of Random House, Inc.,
New York, and simultaneously in Canada by Random House of Canada Limited, Toronto.
Distributed by Random House, Inc., New York.
www.aaknopf.com

Owing to limitations of space, all permissions to reprint previously published material
may be found on pages 283–84.

Knopf, Borzoi Books, and the colophon are registered trademarks of Random House, Inc.

Library of Congress Cataloging-in-Publication Data
Appel, Alfred.
Jazz modernism : from Ellington and Armstrong to Matisse and Joyce / Alfred Appel, Jr.
p.   cm.
Includes index.
ISBN 0-394-53393-3 (alk. papaer)
1. Jazz — History and criticism.   2. Music and literature — History — 20th century.
3. Art and music — History — 20th century.   I. Title.
ML3506 .A66 2002
781.65'3 — dc21   2002066132

Manufactured in Spain

FIRST EDITION

To Nina—the rhythm section

Contents

Jazz Modernism

2. Herman Leonard, *Jo Jones,* Birdland, New York, 1950.

3. Henri Matisse, *Interior with a Violin Case*, Nice, 1918–19.

4. Alexander Calder dancing with Margaret French to the out-of-sight polka riffs of his wife, Louise, doing her Buster Keaton impersonation at the home of the art critic, curator, and collector James Thrall Soby, who took this photograph in 1936. Any photo of an accordion is timeless and excellent grist for a before-and-after sequence.

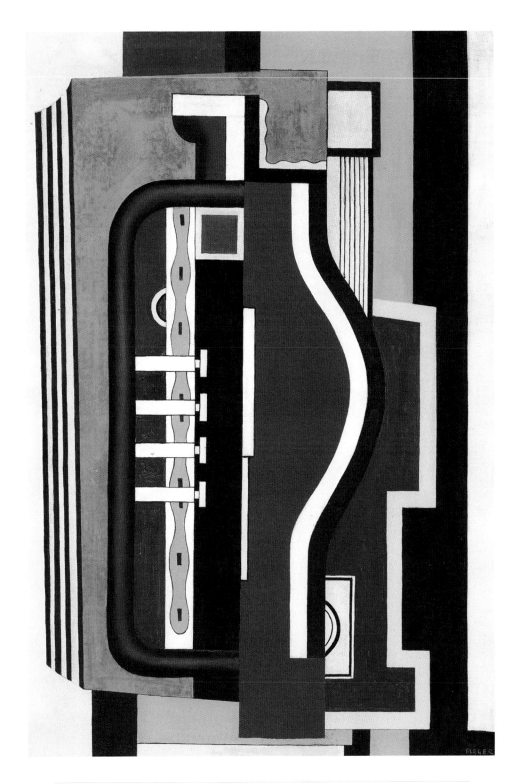

5. Fernand Léger, *Accordion,* 1926, a profile of transformation—the shared chord in these pages.

6. Fernand Léger, *Disks,* 1918.

I

Jazznocracy

This book seeks to establish the place of classic jazz (1920–50)—especially Louis Armstrong, Duke Ellington, Fats Waller, Billie Holiday, Jack Teagarden, and Charlie Parker—in the great modernist tradition in the arts. George and Ira Gershwin should also be in the immediate foreground, partly because they set a swift, efficient pace for readers: "I got rhythm, / I got music, / I got my man— / Who could ask for anything more?" sang Ethel Merman in the first Broadway production of *Girl Crazy* (1930), stopping the show every night. The song was recorded immediately by Ethel Waters and Kate Smith, black and white benchmarks of tasteful singing. It became a standard overnight, and is alive even now, in part because Ira Gershwin's slangy lyrics avoid rhyme—a fatal Tin Pan Alley trap—and allow the woman of the song to express her unabashed egotism and unqualified satisfaction with an amusing and unusually frank concision. Could Ernest Hemingway and James Joyce ask for anything more? Yes—the assurance that their books would endure and continue to be read one hundred years later.

The millennial blather of 1999 included the selection and publication of lists of the 100 Best in most everything, from athletes to novels. As a longtime university teacher, I was frequently asked, "What will last?" Forced to the wall, I gradually formed a short list of the modern masters who were still definitely holding their own with the educated public. Accessibility turned out to be their common denominator, the paradigmatic success of "I Got Rhythm" holding the key. The title's ungrammatical turn projects the gal's unselfconscious sincerity, which points to the wide vernacular base (from language to popular culture and architecture) shared by artists whose appeal seems steady and assured: Ernest Hemingway, who draws on a high school graduate's vocabulary; F. Scott Fitzgerald, whose dark symbolism in *The Great*

Gatsby (1925) is clear enough, especially the fixing of the 1919 World Series and the spoiled gardens throughout the book; Robert Frost, for his vernacular symbolism, too; Pablo Picasso, whose most forceful representational paintings and sculptures of the 1925–40 period and assemblages and collages across the board have a cartoonlike clarity; Joan Miró, who strove mightily to conflate caricature and a child's vision; Alexander Calder, whose playful forms charm (too easily sometimes?) like idiosyncratic dance routines and children's art; and Henri Matisse, whose colors are as pleasing as music—to indulge a cliché that brings us to musicians of the classic jazz period.

The jazz of Armstrong, Ellington, Waller, et al. is the touchstone of accessibility. To disseminate it as widely as possible, I will treat it as part of mainstream culture rather than as the insular, marginalized province of enthusiastic fans alone. In matters pertaining to race and racial politics, my comparisons and unambiguous assertions should be stimulating if not definitive. A comparison of the ways in which sex is addressed by Armstrong, Waller, Picasso, Miró, Matisse, and James Joyce will extend well beyond the purview of jazz. My musical emphasis is on singing and the lyrics of songs, because words lend themselves to discourse more readily than do musical notes: "Singing was more into my blood than trumpet," Armstrong wrote in 1970. As singers, Armstrong, Waller, Teagarden, and Holiday typically had to modify or tear apart and rebuild poor or mediocre Tin Pan Alley material in a procreative manner analogous to the ways in which modernists such as Picasso begot paper collage, wood assemblage, and metal sculpture. "I'm king of the ragpickers!" Picasso proclaimed gleefully around 1930, after he had created *Woman in a Garden,* his first welded tin-and-iron sculpture, proof that machines do not rule (fig. 9). Picasso's proposed memorial to the open-minded poet Guillaume Apollinaire (1928) visualizes a royal ragpicker's best weapon, its two concave frontal wire "feelers" representing a powerful antenna/radar/satellite dish/magnet combination that won't miss a thing, especially since it's grounded by six legs (frontispiece). With or without such divining rods and antennae, a King or Queen of the Ragpickers is a representative figure, confronting and ordering chaos—our goal, simply said, in life if not art. Picasso's royal metaphor is apt here because it gilds the grim reality of the day as documented by Atget (fig. 7). Picasso's classic collage *Guitar, Sheet Music, and Glass*—dated November 18, 1912, diary-style—contains three kinds of rags, of found stuff, and is at once a manifesto, a song, and a strong opening act for this book.

7. Eugène Atget, *Untitled* (ragpicker), Paris, 1899–1900.

8. Pablo Picasso, *Guitar, Sheet Music, and Glass,* November 18, 1912. Pasted paper, gouache, and charcoal.

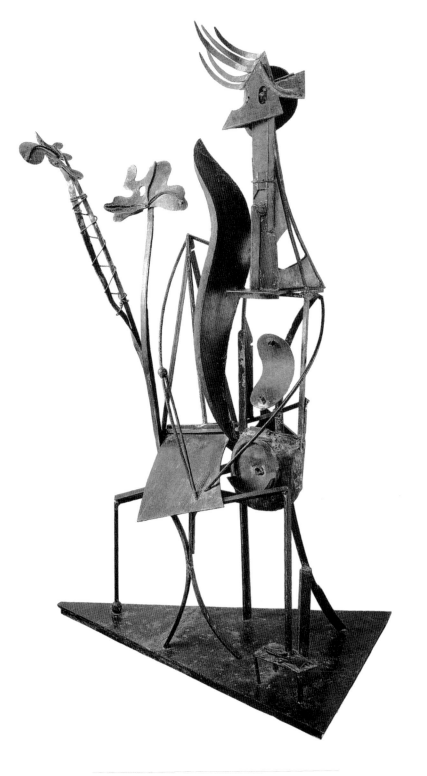

9. Pablo Picasso, *Woman in a Garden*, 1929–30.

LE JOU, the truncated masthead of the newspaper *Le Journal,* leaps out like the advertising on one of the theatrical posters that were so conspicuous on the cluttered outdoor walls and kiosks of Belle Epoque Paris. The headline reads LA BATAILLE S'EST ENGAGÉ, a reference to the start of a battle in the Balkans, the last word excised to emphasize the idea and vernacular metaphor of life as an open-ended series of wars—especially with women, in Picasso's notorious case, as documented early by works such as *Demoiselles d'Avignon* (1907), his nightmare brothel. His truncated JOU announces a course for survival by evoking the verb *jouer,* "to play," "to sport," "to gambol"—excellent if challenging bottom-line advice for any and all battlers, though Picasso himself seems to have followed it happily, on November 18, anyway, given the sunny depths of the two-dimensional collage whose yellowed newsprint and sheet music bits were once an even more optimistic white.

As it happens, the guitar also constitutes a *trompe l'oeil* woman, the turquoise guitar neck serving as an antic but fashionable hat, the white hole as a nose, the wooden hairdo on the left positioned above a black Cheshire cat grin—a cartoon configuration to be sure (Lucy in *Peanuts?*), but hardly a joke inasmuch as the volatile Picasso has achieved a literally perfect balance here between wine, women (he had a new love), and song. The sheet music contains a complementary verbal fragment of song that ends with *"tes bel,"* meaning "thy beautiful"—an adjective that would modify the missing next word. But the lyric fragment suffices since everything before us does harmonize beautifully, in a modernist's unsentimental way. Picasso's JOU dominates BATAILLE—the art of survival.

To call Armstrong, Waller, et al., "modernists" is to appreciate their procedures as alchemists of the vernacular who have "jazzed" the ordinary and given it new life. (In the 1920s the verb *jazz* also meant *fornicate.*) But "modernist" is too broad and loose a term, including as it does T. S. Eliot and Wallace Stevens, among others, who cultivated and collected far fewer rags than Picasso did, and used vernacular lingo

OPPOSITE: 10. Ragpicker's Alchemy. Pablo Picasso, *Baboon and Young,* 1951. Plaster sculpture cast in bronze. 21″ high. The baboon's belly was formed with a ceramic jug, the ears and shoulders with pottery handles, the legs from pieces of wood, the tail from a car's steel spring, the head from toy cars (a Renault and a Panhard) that had been given by Picasso's art dealer, Daniel-Henry Kahnweiler, to the seventy-year-old artist's four-year-old son, Claude.

to connote vulgarity. The tag "Jazz Modernism" has more legs. It is inspired by Matisse's large-format illustrated book titled *Jazz* (1947). He "performed" most of it in 1944, under arduous circumstances during the German occupation of France. Because illness made easel painting difficult, Matisse cut images out of paper and arranged them as collages from which his assistant prepared stencils and then made prints. The twenty images in *Jazz* are nonmusical and unprepossessing subjects drawn principally from the circus and everyday life—e.g., *The Clown* (fig. 14) and *The Swimmer in the Pool* (fig. 101). *Jazz* as a title at once telegraphs a stalwart attitude, constitutes a synonym for "vitality" and "vernacular"—a jazz "Jingle Bells," say—and informs a helpful new generic term. The forms of "Jazz Modernism" may approach abstraction, as in *Jazz,* but the titles affixed to the pictures by the artist should make them accessible, as Matisse's do—a necessity if the art, literature, and music in question are to have a life beyond the classroom and required reading list. There is reason enough to be afraid of James Joyce, and to hope that Apollinaire's dynamically wired antennae system might also stand for our ability to perceive as well as receive.

Ulysses (1922) is the greatest novel of the twentieth century, and was so voted by "a panel of experts" gathered by the Modern Library to select the 100 Best Novels. The victory of *Ulysses* occurred in the wake of my discovery that my long-held projection of a better future for Molly and Leopold Bloom is quite wrong. Aside from Stephen Dedalus, the novel is principally about the Blooms' marital crisis. Bloom is thirty-eight years old, Molly almost thirty-three, but they haven't had complete, successful sexual intercourse for more than ten years, owing to the death of their infant son, or so close readers are led to believe— "we were never the same since," thinks Molly (Modern Library edition, 1961, page 778*). But the famous affirmative prose poetry of Molly Bloom's closing soliloquy, in which she says "yes" eighty-seven times, distributed with musical discretion across her forty-five pages (she's a singer), augurs well for their conjugal future, their marital happiness— or so most of the professors have been telling their students all these years, including Vladimir Nabokov, when he taught at Cornell University (1948–58). But bits and pieces of evidence scattered through *Ulysses* actually indicate that Mr. and Mrs. Bloom will remain sexually

---

* All page citations to *Ulysses* in the present work refer to this edition, still in print.

dysfunctional. Mr. Bloom (as Joyce always calls him, out of respect) is too preoccupied by thoughts of coprolagnia, masochism, sodomy, and anal eroticism, as when he places good-night kisses "on each plump meleneous hemisphere" of Molly's rump (*Ulysses,* page 734). By rereading *Ulysses* with only its problematic sex in mind, determined to connect all the blots, so to speak, I came to the conclusion, after forty years of teaching *Ulysses,* that vaginal intercourse is simply repugnant to Bloom—out of the question. Some schools of thought would rule him a repressed homosexual. The road to truth is a long one. Nor is this jazz modernism.

As for the students, thirty years ago I began an annual prize competition to see if anyone could identify any of the twenty-eight writers of English prose, from the Anglo-Saxons through the Victorians, who are parodied in Joyce's so-called Oxen of the Sun chapter. Not one writer was ever identified by any of the three thousand students, many of them smart indeed, as I could tell from their responses to Joseph Conrad, F. Scott Fitzgerald, Nabokov (*Lolita* but not *Pale Fire*), and Hemingway especially. Hemingway's *The Sun Also Rises* (1926) and *A Farewell to Arms* (1929) found middling to modest spots in the Modern Library's ranking (45 and 72, respectively), but who can doubt why Hemingway continues to hold the attention of enormous numbers of readers? This, from "The Killers" (1927), when they're setting up an ambush in a diner near Chicago, then the jazz as well as crime center of America:

> "Talk to me, bright boy," Max said. "What do you think's going to happen?"
>
> George did not say anything.
>
> "I'll tell you," Max said. "We're going to kill a Swede. Do you know a big Swede named Ole Andreson?"
>
> "Yes."
>
> "He comes here to eat every night, don't he?"
>
> "Sometimes he comes here."
>
> "He comes here at six o'clock, don't he?"
>
> "If he comes."
>
> "We know all that, bright boy," Max said. "Talk about something else. Ever go to the movies?"
>
> "Once in a while."
>
> "You ought to go to the movies more. The movies are fine for a bright boy like you."

For many readers today, such syncopated dialogue beats the rumina-
tions of Stephen Dedalus and Leopold Bloom.

The appeal of Hemingway's jazz modernism is not a simple matter.
His repetition of the physical verbs "come" and "go" make everything
seem to move or jump, even though the two killers are usually seated or
standing still. The passage's withering "bright boy" sounds twenty-
nine times in the short span of six pages, like an angry drum rimshot or
a "bomb," as the bebop drummers of the atomic era, 1945 on, would
term their signature idiosyncrasy, delivered by the left hand—a loud,
sometimes jarring asymmetrical thump that interrupts and plays off
the sizzling forward flow sustained on the large ride cymbal by the
right hand, creating rather than releasing considerable but exhilarating
tension. The story's heady syncopated prose is morally equivocal, bifurcated, and polyrhythmic in the sense that it points to two Heming-
ways: first, the assertively manly male, who walked in the tracks of Al
and Max as an aficionado of the bull ring and killer of big game and, as
a combat journalist in Spain and World War II, was drawn compulsively to the dangers of war; and, second, the refined artist, heir of both
Flaubert and Mark Twain, who lifts us in "The Killers" with his rat-a-
tat-tat prose. The reader also senses that such a runaway pulse alone
could kill you soon enough.

"Rhythm Saved the World" is the title of a 1936 Armstrong number, and it summarizes the cardiovascular truth and root appeal of
poetry, music, and dance indulged sensibly. Machines save the world
and run rhythmically, states Fernand Léger in *Disks* (1918), the artist's
horrific experiences in World War I notwithstanding (fig. 6). As for
pacemakers, Jo Jones, the drummer with Count Basie's greatest bands
(1936–48), is, with Big Sid Catlett, the most important drummer of
the classic jazz period (fig. 2). A well-schooled musician, singer, and
excellent tap dancer who could play the piano, the trumpet, and several
kinds of saxophones, Jones was the first jazz drummer to transfer the
basic rhythmic pulse from the bass drum to the hi-hat, the two small
cymbals that are struck by operating a foot pedal. Although Buddy
Rich and Louie Bellson had greater technique than Jones, and Kenny
Clarke was more radical, creating the bebop style out of Jones, Papa
Jo—as he was called—possessed unrivaled imagination, developed by
necessity in the 1920s, when, in addition to jazz, he also worked in
vaudeville, carnival, and circus bands, learning how to introduce,
accompany, accent, and improve every kind of act, from knife throwers
to acrobatic, somersaulting dogs. Matisse's *Interior with a Violin Case*

(1918–19) is a good example of a needy case (fig. 3). If the violin is being played (the case is empty), the sonic effect isn't tonic enough for Jo Jones, who is warming up in the adjoining chamber and wants to transfuse and renovate Matisse's wishy-washy interior by defining the curtains, widening the red, making the blacks on the dressing table jump and the eel-like designs really dance, preferably next to a solid blue vista, a more riveting Riviera. This would match or approach the graphically sharp, color-saturated dynamism of Matisse's *Jazz* series, which Jones must see as the chromatic equivalent of so many riffs by Basie's brass and saxophone sections and a more immediate delight than *Interior with a Violin Case.*

"Solid! Took the words right out of my mouth," says Jones, from the wings, where he'll remain throughout this book as an interactive force responsible for accenting the music under discussion and improving the flow of the prose on each page, making it all more accessible—the way rhythm and color make Léger's mandala-like *Disks* meaningful and accessible, even though the picture is abstract and almost totally flat. Pictorial bits of a bridge subliminally lead to the present, to computers and CAT scans and better and better sound systems. *Disks* (of the phonographic sort) will be the operative word throughout these pages, which is why the OKeh label is on its own, displayed as a demotic icon in museumlike exhibition space (fig. 11).

Papa Jo will prevail as he always did because, like Sid Catlett, he could play any style, bebop included. He was always ready to play and never at a loss. "He plays like the wind," someone once said. If he didn't have his drums set up or cased nearby when musicians gathered to jam on short notice in a hotel room or at a party, he'd use his wire brushes on a telephone book placed on the seat of a plain wooden chair. If he didn't have his brushes or sticks at hand, he'd roll up a newspaper tightly and swing no less. Jones is said to have used long spoons and whisk brooms, too. A jazz modernist always makes do, from Hemingway's limited vocabulary to tin can alley, Picasso's hunting ground (fig. 9). Verbal and visual puns are central here because they are philoprogenitive, producing at least two new words or forms where there had been one. Picasso's large frond in the garden is also a seed pod, a womb, a flame, a seal, and it's got rhythm—a litter of new forms, to pun again, a man of litters, Pan searching for tin in the alley, to squeeze out another pun, compulsively, fresh JOUs to replicate Picasso's improvisational zeal. His friend André Salmon watched him at work on this sculpture, rummaging frantically through a pile of iron by the light of the blazing forge and "shaking with Luciferian laughter." *Woman in a Garden* was also proposed and rejected as a monument to Apollinaire, to be placed by his Paris grave.

The procreative spirit of jazz modernism is summarized sweetly by Picasso's *Baboon and Young* of 1951 (fig. 10) and Calder's and Léger's responses to the accordion, the homeliest, worst-sounding instrument, rightly associated with the polka, the squarest dance (figs. 4, 5). Léger's rebuilt *Accordion* (1926), a utopian structure, has dignity, trumpet valves, a conspicuously modeled, trumpetlike pipeline that communicates the idea of warmth (human as well as central heating), and is clearly pregnant with—most anything, including Joe Mooney, the only first-rate jazz accordionist. His best and most famous recording, Vincent Youmans's "Tea for Two" (1946), is a classic example of jazz modernism in the way that singer-instrumentalist Mooney (he also played piano and organ) has rewritten Irving Caesar's sung-to-death 1925 lyrics: "They started to raise a family / But the kids left home at the age of three, / Singing: 'Oolong, / Too much o' that Oolong.' " But sonograms of Léger's pregnant accordion only register terra-cotta pigments—art rather than physical reality.

Accessible art should be disseminated as widely as possible because it is tonic, like plasma or André Derain's great four-by-six-foot rhythmic masterpiece, *The Turning Road, L'Estaque* (1906), whose right-hand tree wants her own dance act, anticipating Josephine Baker (fig. 12). The idea of tonic art is old-fashioned and naive to many, but if art (the word is generic, all-inclusive) isn't uplifting, and nationalism, religion, and Marxism have failed, what then? Are irony and self-help books and Prozac going to prove sufficient? The terra-cotta Pompeiian red color shared by Léger, Derain, Matisse's five-by-six-foot *The Red Studio* (1911, fig. 13), and Ellington's 78-rpm OKeh record label (fig. 11) is open-ended in its vernacular color symbolism since their uniform terra-cotta is the same hue as blood stains, and evokes a telling human mark and numerous metaphors, from "young blood" and the urge to "paint the town red" to fanciful lipstick brands such as Revlon's Cherries in the Snow and Max Factor's Paris Red (really) and the red in Wallace Stevens's "Disillusionment of Ten O'Clock" (1923). There the poet laments that no one in his suburban neighborhood is capable of any intense imagining such as a drunken sailor's dreams of "catch[ing] tigers" in "red weather"—the condition, clearly, in the Fauve color fantasias of Matisse and his real-life painting partner Derain, whose curious cabana-like structure (lower left) could provide shelter in case of

11. 1928 record label.

bad color weather. The peasant at center foreground seems to be pointing it out for the benefit of strangers. The same cabana appears in the
immediate left foreground of Derain's similar view, titled *Bridge Over
the Riou* (also 1906). It runs out of the image and into the viewer's psychic space—a door into the picture.

Matisse the proverbial tiger carries arbitrary terra-cotta to another
plane in *The Red Studio*. Its saturated, monochromatic terra-cotta red
sets off Matisse's exhibition-quality arrangement of his own art, which
has more weight than the subsumed, transparent pieces of furniture.
(The studio was in fact white.) The six actual Matisses on the wall,
painted between 1906 and 1911, would all become famous masterpieces, making *The Red Studio* even more compelling now; the artist, it
seems, couldn't stand to part with his creations, their sales potential
notwithstanding. Especially conspicuous is *Le Luxe, II* (1908), on the
far right. The title alludes to the famous refrain of Baudelaire's *L'Invitation au voyage* (1855), where the poet longs for a tension-free, perfect
place, a utopia of the spirit where everything is ordered, *"luxe, calme et
volupté."* And the arbitrary terra-cottas in Derain, Dufy, Vlaminck, and
Matisse would confer immortality on these works by self-reflexively
evoking the unweathered red chroma of surviving Greek clayware circa
450 B.C. This Attic identification is probably "Joycean," out of reach,
but the terra-cotta definitely works as vernacular symbolism. The
OKeh label is primed for immortal music, Greek or Saturday Night
Red—good name for a lipstick, at least.

Evidently Matisse's own work inspires the bliss of Baudelaire's ideal
state, to judge by *The Red Studio,* where time is halted—out, gone, dis-
appeared. The pivotal grandfather clock doesn't have hands or chimes.
The rather arch Art Nouveau design of the plant signals that everything here is cultivated, the art and objects arranged more subtly
around the studio in a circle that starts with a circle, the Matisse-
designed plate on the lower left. The table is set for dinner and art, represented by an open box of sharp new crayons to the right of the Matisse
plate. The gleam on the outlined empty glass emphasizes the vessel's
three-dimensionality—extraordinary in so determinedly flat a visual
space—and points to the idea of nourishment in the deepest sense.
Who wouldn't want to stop at this veritable aid station? Derain's terra-

PRECEDING SPREAD: 12. André Derain, *The Turning Road, L'Estaque,* 1906.

13. Henri Matisse, *The Red Studio,* 1911. Identifiable paintings by Matisse are, from left to right: *Large Nude with Necklace* (1911); *Nude with White Scarf* (1909); to the right of the clock, *The Young Sailor II* (1906–7); *Decorative Figure* (1908); and, far right, *Le Luxe II* (1908). In the foreground, Matisse has placed his sculpture *Upright Nude* (1904) amid tendrils of leaves.

14. Henri Matisse, *The Clown,* the opening image of *Jazz,* 1947.

15. Stuart Davis, *Standard Brand,* 1961.

cotta peasants would feel especially at home. The pale yellow slung-back garden chair is there to accommodate "red weather" transfusions and refills. If *The Red Studio* were magically animated, Matisse would sit down on the left, reach for a fresh crayon, and dash off in eight or ten seconds an elegant line drawing of one of the forms before him. "Pull up a chair," to paraphrase *L'Invitation au voyage.* The tonic attraction and thrill of jazz is based on the listener's incorrect assumption that every improvisation is new and unique, the antithesis of our everyday routine. The case for living art rests here. Derain's cabana accepts reservations for two, the capacity of its terra-cotta bunk bed. "Do you allow dogs?" asks a letter-writer. "Only yellow or terra-cotta pets accepted," reads the reply, by e-mail, to improvise and riff like ragpicker Picasso cutting out and pasting down some salvaged bourgeois wallpaper to express his sense of domestic bliss, his lightness of being—"*bel,*" sings Picasso's collage, even if one fails to read its fine print. Picasso's toy cars at once domesticate the idea of the rag and represent every unprepossessing song that Armstrong and Waller tried to bring home to us (fig. 10).

Since no collagist has left a documentary account of his or her instinctive or conscious course of collecting and recomposing ephemera, Waller's recording of "Swingin' Them Jingle Bells" (1936) can serve as an excellent laboratory example of the art of transformation—predicated, obviously, on the fact that most of us are more familiar with the unadulterated "Jingle Bells" than with "Tea for Two" or the sources of Joyce's literary parodies in *Ulysses,* a tee for one. Song lyrics are now in the foreground as primary texts. Joe Mooney's nonsensical "Oolong" (it's amusing if you know it's a type of tea) teasingly reminds us that music is basically nondiscursive, and that good students should devour verbal bodies of clues. In any event, "oo" has a musical life and history of its own.

Waller, a technically prodigious pianist, feigns respectful restraint at the outset of "Swingin' Them Jingle Bells" as his combo takes on the innocuous, culturally sacrosant ditty, composed in 1857. "Don't you swing them jingles, son!" Waller warns, impersonating an officer of the court or a school principal who is also throwing down the gauntlet to His Rhythm (his sextet's primal name). Waller himself immediately rises to the challenge, first playing the tune straightforwardly, in a rollicking, two-handed manner, then improvising on it in a fierce, minimalist style, the run of single notes from his right hand percussive and bright—word-free, unsentimental bells, a clarion tremolo to signal the fun of a sleigh ride. But someone still has to dispatch those lyrics. Waller sings the famous jingle in falsetto, with a comic lisp—"wide" for "ride"—and, upon completion, affects a deep voice, which asks, "What's the matter with him?" "The jingle bells got him," he answers himself. A gruff, bass-toned burst of the lyrics includes "Look-a-here," addressed to his band: it's your turn, he's saying, it's up to the next soloists to release them all from the bells, the deadening spell of old songs. Gene Sedric's bumptious, uninspired tenor saxophone solo doesn't free them, but trumpeter Herman Autrey catches fire and, verbally encouraged by Waller, unleashes a strong solo, sustaining his last two notes for several measures while Waller shouts, "Oh Jingle Bells! Oh Jingle Bells! Yeah, uh! Swing them bells! Oh, mercy!" His syncopated jubilation is fueled by the knowledge that His Rhythm has dismantled the song's snowy genre scene and made first-rate jazz with what's left. "That's what I'm talkin' 'bout!" Waller declares triumphantly as they ride out the rejuvenated Christmas chestnut, a "Jingle Bells" for all seasons. "Make it new," as Ezra Pound urged American poets in 1914. " 'Tain't what you do, it's the way that you do it," as Trummy Young sang with Jimmie Lunceford's band in 1939. "Jingle Bells" is now as buoyant as a Calder mobile or the floating black "Pad" (hip argot for apartment) in Stuart Davis's *Standard Brand* (fig. 15). Waller and Benny Goodman's 1935 rescue operation helped make "Jingle Bells" the Christmas song most favored by jazz musicians.

Waller and his band are the corkscrew black flame on the left edge of Matisse's *The Clown,* the opening image and pilot light in *Jazz* (fig. 14), where Matisse gives ostensibly banal subjects new life and truly makes light of black in seventeen of the book's twenty images, turning deathly black into something as affecting as a bright color when by definition it doesn't have chroma. Black was already a quietly radical presence in Matisse's *Interior with a Violin Case,* where various blacks—violin case, chair, blotter, inkwell, mirror, and black-edged red footrest—all combine to anchor the timorous room. Ellington's title "Black Beauty" is of course resounding, including as it does the rhetoric of the 1960s.

Fats Waller really is talking about talk, about the divestiture and conversion of language-bound song into pure music, the course followed by Stuart Davis in *Standard Brand* (1961), as he moves from clear, legible words to the nondiscursive, musical or choreographic nature of almost illegible single words. Davis, who usually listened to jazz while he painted (he named his son after the jazz pianist Earl

16. The Oriental Theater, Chicago, 1940. Louis Armstrong Archives, Queens College, City University of New York.

17. Miguel Covarrubias, "Impossible Interview: Fritz Kreisler vs. Louis Armstrong," *Vanity Fair,* February 1936.

Hines), spells "COMPLET" in the French manner to acknowledge his indebtedness to School of Paris art, the cut-ups of Picasso and Matisse's *Jazz* caprices in particular. The less legible white script reads "any," a virtual mantra in Davis's pictures of the time (fig. 15). It abbreviates "anything"—Guillaume Apollinaire's open-ended apostrophe to writers and artists and musicians to be alert to everything, standard brands and low songs especially—"a thousand miscellaneous [urban] items," he declared in his poem "Zone" (1913), a kind of manifesto to Cubists and the first creators of aleatory music, where any sound is judged to have musical potential and value. Picasso's proposed monument to Apollinaire, with its antennae (frontispiece), clearly objectifies "Zone"—and Davis's urban beat, too. The barely legible vertical green "Stuart," top right, one half of the artist's regular signature, is jitterbugging with the inarticulate graphic black symbol for "plus," thereby completing the divestiture and glossing the electric impact of jazz on Davis, a fixture on the New York jazz scene whose painting students included jazz musicians as well known as clarinetist Pee Wee Russell and drummer George Wettling. As in Matisse's *Jazz,* the saturated opaque colors of Davis sound like jazz-bound instruments rather than the translucent chamber music of *Interior with a Violin Case*—its quavering graphic lines choreographed to complement the immaculate bridal curtains. Even if Davis's elevated "Pad" doesn't alert the viewer to the idea of a jazz environment, the entire composition should communicate the essence of classic jazz: joys for everyone, this accessible literary pun thrown in out of goodwill, the bottom line in Waller and Armstrong et al., to use a potential low pun that would have brightened their eyes.

Waller's deconstruction (as some would call it) of "Jingle Bells" is representative Waller and also resembles Armstrong's basic attack on words, which, whatever one thinks the lyrics mean, must first be taken at face value, literally—his persona, the stumbling block posed by Armstrong the singer and stage performer. Rarely does a trumpeter or anyone else in an Armstrong concert venture to sing like him, probably for the same reason that many intelligent critics and historians have downplayed or ignored his immensely influential singing: they regret or deplore its physical side (grinning, mugging, body English) as an embarrassment. Seeing him in an old movie, *High Society* (1956), they wince once again. Armstrong's singing, it is commonly believed, was an anachronistic extension of nineteenth-century minstrelsy's "darky entertainer"—Miguel Covarrubias's 1936 view of him, or so it would seem at first wince from the dialogue in the original caption ("Yo' sendin' me, man") to Armstrong's grotesquely caricatured eyes, lips, teeth, and apelike hand, which is twice the size of Fritz Kreisler's (fig. 17). The caricature turns out to be splendid because it at once embodies an audience's perception of the "darky" persona and hints at the Armstrong whose singing is a powerful musical and spiritual transformation of the minstrel tradition, which should be summarized.

"That's Why Darkies Were Born," a pseudo-spiritual sung fervently by Frank Munn (a white man) in the Broadway revue *George White's Scandals of 1931,* explains that "Some had to slave and be able to sing," which has the virtue of concision. If Munn were black, he might appreciate that the song is in the third person, as opposed to the more demeaning first person, as was the case with the popular "Shine," written in 1924. "Shine" denotes a shoe-shine boy, and a shiny, integratiating smile, and the vernacular verb, synonymous with Uncle Tomming, used by blacks only, as in, "No, I *ain't* shinin'." Colored boys of any age in the twenties, thirties, and forties might be called "shine," sometimes as benignly as all Pullman porters were called "George." And black performers of the day were routinely expected to sing songs such as "Shine," which is in the tradition of the nineteenth-century coon or minstrel song, usually sung by whites or Negroes in burnt-cork blackface.

Armstrong recorded the song in 1931; the Mills Brothers in 1932, with Bing Crosby, a jazz-inflected singer then, whose condescending patter goes with the territory; and Dooley Wilson and John Bubbles sang it stirringly in *Casablanca* (1942) and *Cabin in the Sky* (1943) respectively. Although "Shine" offers one of Armstrong's most brilliant trumpet solos, it is omitted from the ambitious Armstrong anthology, *Louis Armstrong: Portrait of the Artist as a Young Man, 1923–1934,* a 1994 set of four compact discs from Columbia, containing eighty numbers. This excision limns perfectly the custodial impulse to put Armstrong the trumpeter on a pedestal in a well-lit pristine space quite removed from the jungle of race and popular entertainment.

Armstrong's movie rendition of "Shine," in a short film called *A Rhapsody in Black and Blue* (1932), is demeaning enough to symbolize the well-paid black performer's plight and challenge in the thirties. There are two stills from the film in the illustrated catalog of *Louis Armstrong: A Cultural Legacy,* edited by Marc H. Miller (1995), and an excerpt from the movie is included in the 1988 video *Satchmo.* A lazy black cleaning man has been knocked out by his wife and now dreams of himself as emperor of the jungle court of Jazzmania, where none other than Armstrong himself, dressed in a (royal?) leopard skin, plays and sings "Shine" (more about the number later) while standing amid great bubbling soapsuds where one might expect studio-spun clouds—a "joke" about his putative floor-scrubbing and Negro domestic service in general. In another movie, *Going Places* (1938), stableboy Armstrong sings "Jeepers Creepers" to a horse, which may be preferable to Bill "Bojangles" Robinson's turn as Shirley Temple's butler in *The Little Colonel* (1935), since horses can't give orders. Lena Horne and the great tapdancing Nicholas Brothers, Fayard and Harold—"a class act"—were usually confined in movies to a self-contained sequence that could be edited out of films bound for Southern theaters. "All Dark People Is Light on Their Feet" was written by Richard Rodgers and Lorenz Hart as a feature for the Nicholases in their first Broadway musical comedy, *Babes in Arms* (1937), which introduced "My Funny Valentine," "The Lady Is a Tramp," and "Where or When," and was choreographed by George Balanchine, who esteemed the brothers. They were appalled by "their" song, pleaded to have the "is" changed to "are," but to no avail. In the movie *The Great American Broadcast* (1941), they danced as railroad station redcaps. This "cultural legacy" is heavy baggage indeed. In 1971, the year of his death, between performances at the Waldorf-Astoria in New York, his final engagement, Armstrong recalled gravely what it was like in 1933, "in Oklahoma, with two thousand dollars in my pocket and nowhere to eat."

Ellington's assertive "Black Beauty" title of 1928 plays off the visual and verbal cartooning that consistently characterized African-American figures in those years. "A jungle dance in its wilder manifestations, the Lindy Hop is best done to swing music," reads the caption under a photo of two well-dressed black dancers in a *LIFE* magazine picture story on the Savoy Ballroom in Harlem. "As unselfconscious in their kissing as in their dancing, Savoy customers seek no secluded corners for their fun," states a caption beneath a couple snuggling (not kissing) on a Savoy bench (*LIFE,* December 14, 1936). What's in a name? Armstrong and Fats Waller starred in the 1929 all-colored (the nomenclature of the day) Broadway revue *Hot Chocolates* (music by Waller, lyrics by Andy Razaf) while Benny Carter, whose dignity matched his great talents as an arranger and instrumentalist, led a recording group in the thirties and forties with a varying all-star personnel always named the Chocolate Dandies. This was the epoch, after all, when Joe Louis was known as "the Brown Bomber," "the Dark

18. Man Ray, *Noir et blanche,* 1926.

19. Paul Colin, Josephine Baker doing the Charleston, in *Le Tumulte noir*, 1927.

20. Fats Waller and jitterbug pupil, transatlantic liner, 1939.

21. Man Ray, *Self-Portrait*, c. 1921.

Destroyer," "the Sepia Slugger," and "the Tan Tornado." The truly cartoonish name of the Ink Spots, a popular black singing group, may
raise hackles today, but ethnic affrontery of an indiscriminate sort was
the rule in America. Joe DiMaggio's Yankee teammates called him "the
Big Daig" (dago) and an admiring cover story on DiMaggio in *LIFE,*
the most popular magazine of the time, observed, "Instead of olive oil
or smelly bear grease he keeps his hair slick with water. He never reeks
of garlic and prefers chicken chow mein to spaghetti. Like Heavyweight Champion Louis, DiMaggio is lazy, shy and inarticulate" (May
1, 1939). Why wouldn't Bing Crosby, who recorded a memorable "St.
Louis Blues" with Ellington's band in 1932, appear in minstrel blackface in the same year's music short *Dream House?* Armstrong and Waller
thrived in this environment by turning the minstrel tradition upside
down, without bitterness, of course, since they wanted "to bring joy"—
also Brancusi's stated goal—and "make people happy," as Armstrong
said.

Armstrong's greatness as a man and an artist is predicated on the
way he slipped the yoke or prison of show-business negritude and
the cult of the primitive, which are often discussed loosely as one and
the same when in truth they are quite distinctive. The generalized
Romantic/racial idea of the vitalism of the black person is communicated charmingly by the 1939 photograph of Fats Waller trying to
teach an anchored Englishwoman to jitterbug (fig. 20). Meanwhile, in
Paris, Constantin Brancusi had recently sculpted *King of Kings (Spirit of
the Buddha)* in an African style. He was in the first wave of modernists
who, in the early decades of the century, submitted themselves to the
spell of Oceanic and African tribal art as part of an across-the-bored
effort to revitalize fettered and supposedly moribund Europe. Apollinaire's tiny emblematic face atop a pole clearly replicates an African
grave marker because Picasso deems the dead poet magisterially
"African" in his totally open, unrestricted sense of the potential raw
materials of art (frontispiece). A tribal fetish figure, for instance, could
be studded with hundreds of nails, shells, small blades, pretty stones,
feathers, beads, and bits of clothing, each representing a village peti-
tioner's fervent wish or prayer—"Free the Caucasian," say.

Africanesque Brancusi sculptures titled *Adam and Eve, Socrates, The
Little French Girl,* and *Spirit of the Buddha* (figs. 31, 30, 32) together
define the breadth of the perceived cultural malaise and the role of self-
conscious primitivism as plasma—"self-conscious" because it was the
product of educated, independent, ego-driven "red weather" artistic

choice rather than a selfless village artisan's efforts to meet the religious/ceremonial needs of his tribal community. Brancusi's friend Man Ray could thus pose his notoriously free-spirited mistress Kiki as a Brancusi face/ovoid holding an African mask—the id, no doubt, in this contrived, "civilized" context, every hair in place (fig. 18). Yet it's too small to cover her face—and needs? But if a phallic symbol is defined as an object taller than it is wide, then its erectness should be sufficient. *Noir et blanche* ("Black and White"), as Ray titled it, subliminally reinforces a very primitive canard.

Show-business primitivism, often the setting for Ellington and Armstrong (i.e., Jazzmania), is usually an off-key mélange of kitsch and creativity, as in Josephine Baker's fabled 1925 run in Paris's *La Revue nègre,* whose sets were designed by Covarrubias, one featuring huge vegetables and ripe fruits. Baker famously danced in a sarong of (phallic) bananas. Paul Colin caricatured her respectfully throughout most of his 1927 portfolio of lithographs, *Le Tumulte noir* (reprinted in 1998), but his image here of Baker dancing the Charleston represents the most condescending and dehumanizing racist side of negrophilia (fig. 19). Colin's caged creature is levitating because "All Dark People Is Light on Their Feet." The song title alone bespeaks the most conspicuous contemporary incarnation of primitivism, NBA basketball, athleticism truly beyond human reach: Michael Jordan's most frequent partner on TV commercials in the year 2000 was Bugs Bunny, his possible NBA replacement represented by a cartoon kangaroo atop a basketball net. The hoop film *White Men Can't Jump* (1992) only rephrases Rodgers and Hart's racialist message with a "liberal" wink that nonetheless endorses the potentially compromising primitivist ideal of supreme black potency. *English Girls Can't Dance* could be a Monty Python movie, and *White Men Can't Swing* is an apt alternate title for Man Ray's *Self-Portrait* (circa 1921), where he posits a life-support system for self-conscious primitivists: a little cymbal attached to a phonograph machine, enabling an effete "drummer," the anti–Jo Jones, to accompany wild music and at least produce dynamic, openmouthed shadows—a rare joke at the expense of the civilized primitivist, executed as lightly as a Josephine Baker levitation (fig. 21). Jokes aside, we are fortunate in 2002 if someone can simply recommend or prescribe "red weather" jazz that will levitate us, figuratively or literally.

The size of Armstrong's name suspended above Chicago's Oriental Theater at once measures the popularity he enjoyed as an entertainer during his lifetime and his stature today as an American classic (fig. 16), the only jazz musician who is securely in the canon, ensconced as firmly as Hemingway, Faulkner, and Fitzgerald. (Duke Ellington is there as a composer). The humorous promise of Miguel Covarrubias's 1936 "Impossible Interviews" caricature in *Vanity Fair* turns on the distance between "high" and "low" music. ("Impossible Interviews," a popular feature for two years, typically brought together Stalin and John D. Rockefeller in one drawing and Freud and Jean Harlow in another.) Here, classical violinist Fritz Kreisler has switched to piano and sheet music after breaking a string trying to jam with tense Louis Armstrong, who literally has no ear—for classical music? The humor, such as it is, is no doubt lost or dulled today by the frequency with which opera stars sing pop, jazz virtuosi appear as guest soloists with symphony orchestras, and by the institutional respect accorded jazz. *Everyone* now seems to have "big ears," the highest compliment a jazzman could receive in the argot of the 1940s—the possible source and meaning of Calder's 1943 piece of radar, *The Big Ear,* a huge crescent-moon "antenna." Large-eared Lincoln Center now has its own Jazz Orchestra, an impossibility twenty years ago. A vast Louis Armstrong Archives has been established at Queens College, City University of New York. An exhibition called "Louis Armstrong: A Cultural Legacy," organized by the Queens Museum and the Smithsonian Institution, toured the country for two years and completed its run in 1996 with a signal installation at the National Portrait Gallery in Washington, D.C. None of this will surprise those younger readers who never pause over the fact that their favorite rappers and rock-'n'-rollers are all called "artists" just as readily as the journalists who cover them are billed as "critics." "What *isn't* art?" is now a challenging, defining question for a culture that, for better or worse, has all but eliminated the distinctions between "high" and "low" art. "Low," a collective entity, made distinctions, too, especially in the marketing of jazz.

OKeh Records, subsequently a subsidiary of Columbia, was interested in sales, not art, when it signed Armstrong in late 1925 to record under his own name for the first time on their "race" series, aimed solely at black audiences. The term "race" was synonymous with "Negro" and "colored"—"The World's Greatest Race Artists" proclaimed an OKeh magazine ad in 1925, a great year in the arts. It saw the publication of *The Great Gatsby,* Hemingway's *In Our Time,* Cather's *The Professor's House,* and Alain Locke's anthology, *The New Negro: Voices of the Harlem Renaissance,* which were not raised in praise of lowly jazz, where song titles alone could be embarrassing. The third recording ses-

sion of Armstrong's Hot Five, in February 1926, his most prolific, produced six numbers, most significantly "Heebie Jeebies," "Cornet Chop
Suey," and "Georgia Grind"—his initial vocal, a double entendre (a
dance move and fornication). Pianist Lil Hardin, soon to become Armstrong's second wife (and a stabilizing force), sings first, choreograph-
ing the grind: "Shake it to the east / Shake it to the west," lines used in
at least a hundred other ignoble songs. Armstrong follows her and sings
unmemorably about a sick old lady who, like everybody else, "went
crazy 'bout the Georgia Grind"—lyrics to remind us that the art in this
music evolved from below, wondrously. "Cornet Chop Suey," Armstrong's first instrumental showcase, aspires to art, though Armstrong
would never have used the word. Its title announces that it's pure self-
expression, forget about his urban audience—working-class blacks,
part of the Great Migration from the South, a flight from "medieval
America to modern" and a "more democratic chance," as Alain Locke
characterized it in *The New Negro*. The executives at OKeh Records sur-
mised that the migrants wanted good-time music, or stuff that imi-
tated their lives more directly, and withheld "Cornet Chop Suey" for
several months, preferring to release "Heebie Jeebies," which offers
Armstrong's first scat singing, not by definition an accessible form.

Scat, a virtually wordless jabberwocky, thought by some scholars to
have its origins in African incantation rites and rituals, came to Armstrong from the vernacular art performed by vocal quartets on the New
Orleans streetcorners of his youth. The term *heebie-jeebies* is even more
immediate, having just entered the vernacular around 1925 through its
use by Billy DeBeck in his widely syndicated comic strip *Barney Google*.
Webster's *Third International Dictionary* defines *heebie-jeebies* as "a tense,
nervous, jumpy condition"; "jangled nerves" "sometimes marked by
hallucinations," a particularly relevant characterization, given Armstrong's black constituency, many of whom still trafficked in old down-
home Negro superstitions and folk beliefs in voodoo, witchery, spells,
devils, demons, and hauntings, and there's no reason to think that
Armstrong didn't take them seriously, too. "Yes, Mama, Papa's got the
heebie-jeebies," sings Armstrong. The lyrics are simple and repetitive,
but they must be reckoned with to understand how the performer may
serve the community as shaman. (Writers on Armstrong never pay
attention to his lyrics.) "Don't be blue / Someone with juju / Come on
an' do that thing," he sings, addressing his black audience intimately
enough since few African-Americans today can translate or define
"juju." Webster's *Third* (always try there first) on *juju:* "a fetish, charm,

or amulet of West African tribes"; "the magic attributed to the use of a juju." They should also have said it was a synonym for *voodoo* among American blacks.

Instead of chasing away the heebie-jeebies with an aggressive trumpet solo, his defense in subsequent numbers ("The Skeleton in the Closet," 1936), Armstrong answers these fears with a good-humored scat chorus, equal to bright whistling or tapdancing by a graveyard. Its comprehensible opening phrase "East side" (followed by the swallowed word "west") fixes the heebie-jeebies on the map. Armstrong articulates "deep down, deep down" as he tests the lower (lowest?) register of his gravelly scat, suppressing a chuckle as he discovers his full range— Hemingway's triumph of the same time, with "The Killers" and his first novel, *The Sun Also Rises*. After Armstrong's scat chorus, and Lil Hardin's stiff piano solo, the ensemble rides out the number, New Orleans style. "What you doin' with the heebies?" asks another musician as they conclude, though the answer is already self-evident: laughing in the heebies' faces, achieving a comic catharsis or exorcism ("do that thing") that anticipates Armstrong's triumph in "Shine." Armstrong is signifying "safe transport home," to put it in words, which neither Armstrong nor his audience required. "Heebie Jeebies" was a great hit, Armstrong's first, selling forty thousand copies in three weeks (a total sale of ten thousand was deemed a success). "Make it new," Ezra Pound had said, and Armstrong did, giving body and depth to streetcorner jive.

Armstrong atop the Oriental sounds racial, sexual, and aggressive, and should, since his name has usurped that of the film title and Burgess Meredith, the white star of *San Francisco Docks,* the movie then showing at the Oriental, for integrated audiences—nothing to take for granted in 1940, only four years after Armstrong got his first character role, in a Bing Crosby movie, *Pennies from Heaven,* where he was the first black to share top, equal billing with whites. He also received equal billing with Frances Langford and Crosby on a special twelve-inch 78-rpm record of the film's music (soundtrack albums were unheard of). Teddy Wilson joined the Benny Goodman Trio that year, 1936, making it the first integrated jazz group to perform in public on a regular basis. The integration of organized baseball was ten years in the future. Jazz led the way, and still can, if the correct information about the truly hybrid nature of jazz can be disseminated, absorbed, and accepted.

Since jazz is played everywhere around the world, it has evolved naturally into a multicultural art, one quite independent of any program. The designation "multicultural" by no means diminishes the African-American core of jazz, nor the historical fact that the principal players on every instrument have been black, with the exception of Benny Goodman on clarinet (some would say Artie Shaw) and Jack Teagarden on trombone (the pre-1950 period). Goodman's famous tag, "King of Swing," a fair assessment of his technical skills, was the product of publicity, but it rankles even today, and is cited as the essence of cultural presumption and the appropriation of "Black Beauty" (Ellington's title). The parenthetical Spanish translation of Ellington's song on the OKeh label, *Belleza Negra,* identifies the record as an export item that documents the international appeal of jazz as of 1928 (fig. 11).

American ragtime, first cousin of jazz, composed by whites and blacks, captivated Paris as early as 1911, its syncopations informing the pulsating pictures of ragtime devotees Sonia and Robert Delaunay and Gino Severini, whose *The Bear Dance at the Moulin Rouge* (1913) celebrates the provocative, bodies-rubbing-together "grizzly bear" dance that Vernon and Irene Castle had introduced in Paris in 1912. Their accompanying ragtime band was evidently less wild than Severini's, where his dancers' feet have been beared (fig. 23)—a hairier atavism than Josephine Baker's (fig. 19) or Picasso's woman (fig. 33). The Castles' historically important transformation of genteel American dance points ahead to eclectic performers such as Fred Astaire (fig. 24), who played Vernon Castle in the 1939 film, and the Nicholas Brothers, who also blended tap and jazz and ballroom and ballet, black and white without grays, the stylized dress and Art Deco scheme of Astaire and his 1930s movie sets—grace under no pressure, unless you call Astaire "multicultural" too casually.

Because race-based politics and programs thrive on differences, academic multiculturalists would discourage the idea of jazz as multicultural. To discover whether a critic or cultural historian is concerned primarily with art or racial politics, see what they say about Bix Beiderbecke's influence, and how quickly they gainsay the genius of George Gershwin and Astaire, downgrading their accomplishments as exploi-

OPPOSITE: 22. "The music [jazz] evolved from below, wondrously." Constantin Brancusi's studio, Paris, c. 1923, photographed by Brancusi, who posits a veritable "Georgia Grind" with raw materials, the head in the foreground, overturned monumental cup (right), and accidental spotting on the photo representing his struggle to refine such raw stuff.

23. Gino Severini, *The Bear Dance at the Moulin Rouge,* 1913, a distillation of sexuality, movement, musical vitality, and Severini's energy that brings to mind W. B. Yeats's line "How can we know the dancer from the dance?" (from "Among School Children," 1928).

24. The Jazz Dance: Fred Astaire and Rita Hayworth in the film *You Were Never Lovelier* (1942, music by Jerome Kern, lyrics by Johnny Mercer), performing "The Shorty George," an eccentric jazz step of the day named after its supposed creator, a champion dancer at Harlem's Savoy Ballroom. Count Basie had already composed and recorded his own "Shorty George" in 1938. Photo: John Florea / TimePix.

25. The No Airs Dance: Astaire elevates Ginger Rogers and himself in *Carefree* (1938, music and lyrics by Irving Berlin) in their number "The Yam," a screwball dance and song that recommends a "yam session"—hot sweet potatoes, hoofing, and jazz that will "shake your Depression." The number undermines the duo's dignified, formal dress—talent, you see, defines aristocracy.

26. Alex Steinweiss designed this *Boogie Woogie* cover, 1942, an album in the record collection of Piet Mondrian. Steinweiss virtually invented the designed album cover in 1939, an unappreciated achievement.

tations of black sources. Cornetist Beiderbecke, the first major white soloist to develop independent of black sources, and his bandmate Frank Trumbauer, influenced countless black musicians, especially the tenor saxophonist Lester Young and the subsequent "cool school" of jazz, black and white. (Miles Davis acknowledged Beiderbecke's influence by way of the Bix-inflected Bobby Hackett.) Gershwin's example makes a powerful if not definitive case for jazz and dance as a racial two-way street or river of inspiration and influence. Gershwin certainly drew on African-American musicians but in turn became "White Heat" (a Will Hudson number), as composer and pianist, a rich lode for black musicians, who quite naturally played the best songs by the best white songwriters—it wasn't a political issue. Even Miles Davis, a racially proud man, recorded instrumental selections from Gershwin's *Porgy and Bess* in 1958 (arranged by Gil Evans, a white man), notwithstanding its controversial book and (coon show?) libretto. Simply enough, the words didn't matter.

Only the blues exceeds Gershwin's "I Got Rhythm" as the most pervasive harmonic progression in jazz. Armstrong's 1931 large ensemble version of the recently composed "I Got Rhythm" ends uniquely for him with some almost frantic collective improvisation by the entire band, "gots" amuck—acknowledging the song's rich potential, it would seem, and splendid avatars, from Count Basie's "Lester Leaps In" (1939) and Ellington's "Cottontail" (1940) to Dizzy Gillespie's "Salt Peanuts" (1945), Thelonious Monk's "52nd Street Theme" (1945) and "Rhythm-A-Ning" (1957), and some dozen compositions by Charlie Parker, including "Moose the Mooche" (1946) and "Constellation" (1948). The greatest "I Got Rhythm" issued under its own title was recorded "live" by a racially mixed group, the Benny Goodman Quartet (1938, at Carnegie Hall). On Fats Waller's version (1935), clarinetist Rudy Powell opens his solo by quoting "Yankee Doodle Dandy"— musical shorthand that declares the Gershwin number a pan-racial treasure in every town of the union. The out-of-scale white and black jazz hands of Covarrubias's caricature become surreal but equal partners in Alex Steinweiss's cover design for the 1942 *Boogie Woogie* album (fig. 26) on which black and white players—pianist Albert Ammons and trumpeter Harry James—do play together as a duo on two hard-swinging numbers, "Boo-Woo" and "Woo-Woo" (1939), which were among the discs that Mondrian listened to in New York while composing his greatest works, *Broadway Boogie Woogie* (1942–43) and *Victory Boogie Woogie,* left unfinished at his death in 1944 (figs. 41, 42).

Parker was a bona fide multiculturalist long before the politically charged word was coined. Tales abound to reinforce the point. How he moved Texas roustabouts, cowboys, and rough women when he sat in with a country-and-western band in a Dallas roadhouse and played "Home on the Range" straightforwardly, as a dirge—"sounding like a bagpipe," according to the bass player Gene Ramey. Or how well he jammed in Montmartre with gypsy musicians, playing their own songs. Or how his extroverted, staccato solos inspired the mainly Hispanic rumba and mambo dancers at Roseland Ballroom on Broadway when he appeared as guest soloist with Machito's Afro-Cuban Orchestra, as the Havana-born leader billed his popular New York–based Latin band. This was in 1948 or 1949, when Parker was promoting "Okiedoke" and "Mango Mangue," two of his most commercially successful numbers, which he'd recently recorded with Machito. The record company's hyphenated multicultural marking and marketing of a bebop star created some bitter controversy among jazz purists, white and black alike. When disc jockey "Symphony Sid" Torin interviewed Parker on the radio, the saxophonist sailed over the grounds of the argument. "It's all music, man," he said. "Just call it music," he quietly insisted. Beiderbecke and Trumbauer have red and green complexions on the 1947 album cover, arbitrary pan-racial choices that reflect commercial designer Jim Flora's devotion to his fine-arts sources, Joan Miró and Paul Klee (fig. 27). It's all art, man. Parker's ethic and aesthetic make him *King of Kings,* to appropriate the title of Brancusi's sculpture rather than toy with Benny Goodman's advertising. Goodman, in turn, was part of Brancusi's musical life. His records are included in the sculptor's surviving collection, which contains many first-rate jazz discs such as Don Redman's instrumental "I Got Rhythm" (1931) and Ellington's "Harlem Speaks" (1933). If Brancusi had titled at least two works after these numbers, we'd be sure that he carved to jazz, its beat recorded in the dart and dash of his chisel marks.

A comparison of three examples of Brancusi's pieces of self-conscious primitivism allows us to witness quite literally the kind of multicultural conversion process that defies musical analysis. Seen next to its African source, *The Little French Girl* of 1914–18 is obviously derivative (fig. 30). *Adam and Eve* (1921), however, represents a great advance for the Rumanian-born peasant carver, starting with the idea of Adam on the bottom, supporting an early feminist platform (fig. 31). Brancusi has clearly appropriated and integrated basic African forms in *Adam and Eve,* especially the sawtoothed edges, but Eve's conflated

BIX and TRAM

BIX BEIDERBECKE. WITH FRANKIE TRUMBAUER'S ORCHESTRA

flora

SET C-144 • A HOT JAZZ CLASSIC • #20 IN A SERIES THAT MADE JAZZ HISTORY

COLUMBIA ᴬᴰ RECORDS

27. Jim Flora, album cover, 1947, from the pioneering series of jazz reissues produced by George Avakian for Columbia in the 1940s.

breasts/testicles and neck/penis are improvisations on a Greek theme. In Plato's *Symposium,* Aristophanes tells his companions that there were once three sexes— each shaped like a globe—male, female, and hermaphrodite. Each was split by the king of the gods for behaving badly, and each has ever sought reunion, which Brancusi has achieved here, in the first masterpiece of Afro-Rumanian sculpture, multiculturalism made visible. Self-pollination, the hermaphrodite's choice, it seems, is a saving possibility enjoyed by twenty percent of plants—and by every successful artist, speaking figuratively. Such polymorphous ripeness also applies to Picasso's linear Apollinaire (frontispiece), whose womblike ovoid torso (based on a common African harvest festival fertility figure at right) projects several phallic arms—expressed more subtly than Brancusi's *Adam and Eve* visual double entendres. Eve's vulval lips, seemingly a racial caricature à la Paul Colin (fig. 19), actually look quite all right from other angles. Curiously, there are no female black singers represented in Brancusi's record collection, though Eve's essence is reflected in his discs by amusing icons of female power and brio such as Ethel Merman, Mae West, Carmen Miranda, and Sophie Tucker.

Brancusi, who, unlike Picasso and Derain, kept no tribal artifacts around the studio, then went more than fifteen years without carving in an Africanesque mode before returning to the fold to fashion the ten-foot-high *King of Kings* (circa 1938) with no self-consciousness, it seems, like the King of Swing, Benny Goodman, playing the blues as he felt them, thickening his liquid tone, smearing and slurring notes at will—*his* notes, *his* tone, rather than anything he'd heard on a recording by some Negro player. (Jazz players around the world are still echoing the tones and pet phrases of Armstrong, Gillespie, Parker, and John Coltrane, producing so many *Little French Girls.*) Unlike his friend

---

ABOVE: 28. Ceremonial spoon, Dan tribe, Ivory Coast or Liberia. Wood. 20½″ high. The womblike form was drawn on by many modernists, including Picasso, Miró, Brancusi, and Giacometti.

Léger, who merely perused ethnological textbook drawings for his "primitive" stage designs, Brancusi had finally internalized it all, had become an African, if you will, at age sixty-two—a tribe of one, free to improvise a generalized, almost source-proof work that looks thoroughly African and could be exhibited as such, save for the cartoonish crown (only the serrations of the neck are old hat).

Picasso the improviser arrived at a similar juncture as early as 1908, in the *Nude with Raised Arms,* an intense gouache dashed off in the wake of his *Demoiselles d'Avignon* (fig. 33). But here the twenty-eight-year-old artist isn't in recoil from grotesque, intimidating female forms or unstable, fractured space. He's erotically confident, notwithstanding his low, potentially overwhelming angle of vision. Although the woman's front leg belongs to a quadruped, Picasso himself rather than atavism is the source of vitality here, communicated by the artist's striations and polyrhythmic brushstrokes, akin to the rhythmic chisel marks on Eve's lower lip and the vibrant "mouths" in *Danaïde's* base (fig. 34)—"Swingin' Them Brown Pigments and Blocks of Wood" instead of identifiable tribal forms. As mood music, this says skip the smooching and foreplay. Jo Jones needn't add a beat. In painterly terms, white truly highlights black. Paradoxes abound. Picasso's masklike Africanesque nose shares its space with a naturalistic "Caucasian" mouth, akin to the *King of Kings's* anachronistic crown—a serious self-reflexive joke that breaks the most convincing African spell ever cast by a Western modernist and reminds us that art creates its own reality and issues no passports.

Charlie Parker analogously concludes several fast-paced, hard-swinging numbers circa 1945 by stopping on a dime and quoting—out of tempo, with leisurely elegance—from Percy Grainger's *Country Gardens,* a cartoon crown of musical notes that evokes an English environment at considerable geographic remove from the main locus of the bebop experiment, uptown New York and the clubs of Fifty-second Street. "Koko" (1945), the most famous of Parker's improvisations, quotes part of the clarinet solo from the New Orleans warhorse "High Society" so seamlessly that it appears to be part of Parker's creation rather than a cutting musical anachronism as arbitrary as Picasso's JOU. In "Dexter's Deck" (1945), tenor saxophonist Dexter Gordon interpolates "Sonny Boy," one of Al Jolson's most famous blackface numbers from the twenties; as in Parker, Gordon's manner is not bitter or satiric. Such quotations are frequent in their work, especially in extended "live" recordings, and distinguish Yeats's dancer from the dance. Tenor

29. Helmet mask, Senufo tribe, Ivory Coast. Wood. 39″ high.

30. Constantin Brancusi, *The Little French Girl,* 1914–18. Oak. 4′ high.

31. Constantin Brancusi, *Adam and Eve*, 1921. Chestnut and oak, respectively, on a limestone base. Sculpture approximately 7′ high.

32. Constantin Brancusi, *King of Kings (Spirit of the Buddha)*, c. 1938. Oak. 10′ high.

33. Pablo Picasso, *Nude with Raised Arms,* 1908.

saxophonist Sonny Rollins, influenced by Gordon especially, was soon (1954–58) recording straight-faced and inspired versions of unlikely songs for a Harlemite to choose: "There's No Business Like Show Business"; "I'm an Old Cowhand"; "Wagon Wheels"; "Rock-a-Bye Your Baby with a Dixie Melody"; "Surrey with the Fringe on Top" (from *Oklahoma*); and "Toot Toot Tootsie," which had been sung by Jolson in the first talking picture, *The Jazz Singer* (1927), where he also warbled "Mammy" in blackface. At the height of their revolution and powers, these young bebop modernists were positing a thoroughly American, pan-racial utopia or alternative universe where it's all music, there's room for every sound—all registered by Apollinaire-like antennae (frontispiece)—and nothing that a jazz modernist can't swing, from tinny songs to toy or real cars. Near the end of his life (1955), Parker wanted to study with Edgard Varèse, the French-American composer of aleatory music, whose *Ionisation* (1931) is a sonata for percussion instruments and sirens.

Parker enthusiasts circa 1950 often declared him the jazz equivalent of Stravinsky and Bartók, and asserted that he'd absorbed their music, though skeptics countered that there was no evidence he was even familiar with it. Parker himself clarified the issue for me one night in the winter of 1951, at New York's premier modern jazz club, Birdland, at Broadway and Fifty-second Street. It was Saturday night, Parker's quintet was the featured attraction, and he was in his prime, it seemed. I had a good table near the front, on the left side of the bandstand, below the piano. The house was almost full, even before the opening set—Billy Taylor's piano trio—except for the conspicuous empty table to my right, which bore a RESERVED sign, unusual for Birdland. After the pianist finished his forty-five-minute set, a party of

---

OPPOSITE: 34. "We Got Rhythm" (three voices in the wood)—Constantin Brancusi, *Danaïde*, 1913. Bronze with black patina and gold leaf. Two-part base of limestone and oak. Overall height 4′. The "loud," open "mouths" suggest that the delicate, refined golden girl has a well-concealed lusty side—a Grace Kelly fire-and-ice type. Brancusi often used his bases to carry a countermelody. The titles of the discs in his collection are direct enough, from Mae West's "I Like a Guy What Takes His Time" (1933, as "Lady Lou" in the film *She Done Him Wrong*) to Brancusi's next-to-last record acquisition, made in 1954, three years before his death at age eighty-one: "Thirteen Women and Only One Man in Town," by Bill Haley and His Comets, from the film *Rock Around the Clock*—the new wave, then, of poor white musical primitivism.

four men and a woman settled in at the table, rather clamorously, three
waiters swooping in quickly to take their orders as a ripple of whispers
and exclamations ran through Birdland at the sight of one of the men,
Igor Stravinsky. He was a celebrity, and an icon to jazz fans because he
had sanctified modern jazz by composing *Ebony Concerto* for Woody
Herman and his Orchestra (1946)—a Covarrubias "Impossible Interview" come true.

   As Parker's quintet walked onto the bandstand, trumpeter Red
Rodney recognized Stravinsky, front and almost center. Rodney leaned
over and told Parker, who did not look at Stravinsky. Parker immediately called the first number for his band, and, forgoing the customary
greeting to the crowd, was off like a shot. At the sound of the opening
notes, played in unison by trumpet and alto, a chill went up and down
the back of my neck. They were playing "Koko," which, because of its
epochal breakneck tempo—over three hundred beats per minute on the
metronome—Parker never assayed before his second set, when he was
sufficiently warmed up. Parker's phrases were flying as fluently as ever
on this particularly daunting "Koko." At the beginning of his second
chorus he interpolated the opening of Stravinsky's *Firebird Suite* as
though it had always been there, a perfect fit, and then sailed on with
the rest of the number. Stravinsky roared with delight, pounding his
glass on the table, the upward arc of the glass sending its liquor and ice
cubes onto the people behind him, who threw up their hands or
ducked. The hilarity of the audience didn't distract Parker, who, playing with his eyes wide open and fixed on the middle distance, never
once looked at Stravinsky. The loud applause at the conclusion of
"Koko" stopped in mid-clap, so to speak, as Parker, again without a
word, segued into his gentle version of "All the Things You Are."
Stravinsky was visibly moved. Did he know that Parker's 1947 record
of the song was issued under the title "Bird of Paradise"?

   The mere presence of Red Rodney on the bandstand is worthy of
note because no black leader of small or large bands of that time
(1945–55) used more white musicians than Parker did—"It's all music,
man." (Rodney, Chet Baker, Stan Levey, Teddy Kotick, Joe Albany,
Dodo Marmarosa, and Al Haig, among others.) The interracial compo-
nents of jazz groups and their audiences are of great social significance,
and not likely to be analyzed well, since potential jazz historians and
biographers are deprived of what serious scholars take for granted—a
paper trail of letters, diaries, and so forth. A circa-1944 photo of an
integrated jazz group is particularly inspiring if you remember or have

35. Ben Shahn, *Welders,* 1943.

OVERLEAF: 36. Charlie Parker and Red Rodney, listening to Dizzy Gillespie and bassist Clyde Lombardi (in the mirror), Club Downbeat, New York, 1948. Photograph by William P. Gottlieb.

at hand an anthology of American propaganda posters of the World War II period. Although the ubiquitous posters celebrated the ideals of unity, faith, and freedom, only one seems to have pictured an African-American male—Ben Shahn's *Welders* of 1943 (fig. 35). Millions of people saw it, but Shahn's black welder could still be wondering, "Why is my white brother squeezing me out of the picture?"

The intimate, crowded jazz clubs along Fifty-second Street offered nightly examples of interracial harmony, on and off the bandstand. I want to contribute at least one memorable example in behalf of the unwritten social history of jazz integration. In 1949, shortly after Big Sid Catlett had left Armstrong's All Stars to freelance, I encountered him at Jimmy Ryan's, playing drums in an ad-hoc quartet led by tenor saxophonist Coleman Hawkins. The club was jammed, with quite a few musicians present, Buddy Rich most conspicuously—grinning, snapping his fingers, chewing gum double time, itching to sit in with Hawkins and take on Catlett. After two numbers, Rich was invited up on the tiny bandstand, the immense Catlett bowing with a ceremonious flourish as Rich, a small, wiry man, slipped quickly behind Catlett's drums, made some adjustments, took up the sticks, and nodded to Hawkins *I'm ready.*

Rich's grin expanded, his eyes almost disappearing, as Hawkins began to play a simple "I Got Rhythm" variation known as "Boff Boff," a wry challenge to, and acknowledgment of, Rich's gladiatorial spirit, since this was the riff Armstrong's group used almost every night to set up Big Sid's one featured number, a five-minute drum solo. Hawkins played half a chorus of "Boff Boff," and Buddy was off to the races, the world's greatest white drummer about to outdo Sidney Catlett and the fireworks of Bastille Day as well as the Fourth of July. He ended his ten-minute drum solo by attacking the snare drum, doubling and then tripling the tempo of his long, flawless press roll until his hands were a blur. Done! Enthusiastic applause. Dripping with perspiration, the grinning Rich got up and jumped down like a dismounting jockey and took a seat at a front table.

Catlett took his place behind the drums and verbally set a medium "lope" tempo: "Doo-bow, doo-bow." Hawkins and his bass and pianist played one straightforward chorus of "Honeysuckle Rose" and Hawkins stepped aside, to the left edge of the bandstand. Sid's turn. Hold on to your seats. Grasping the sticks lightly in his Covarrubias hands, Catlett began the snare-drum version of a soft-shoe dance, twirling the sticks in the air to allow measures of silence to pass. Unexpectedly he put down his right-hand stick but kept the rhythm going by switching the right hand's stroke to the foot-pedaled bass drum. Without missing a beat, he reached into his jacket pocket and withdrew a cigarette. He placed it between his lips. Then he pulled out a kitchen match and lit it with a flick of his long thumbnail. The drum solo continued, on automatic pilot. Catlett let the match burn for a moment, a fellow in no hurry, about to enjoy a smoke with his midmorning cup of coffee. The audience was rapt, absolutely silent. Then he lit the cigarette, inhaled deeply, luxuriating in the pleasure, closing his eyes and opening them as he slowly exhaled two matching tusks of smoke. "Sid, you mother-fucker!" yelled Buddy. The audience erupted with laughter, cheers, and applause. Catlett picked up the discarded stick, did a short, fast drum-roll, and Hawkins and the others played the out-chorus blithely, Catlett's one final thump of the bass drum falling exactly with Hawkins's last breathy note. The applause was thunderous.

Buddy Rich leaped up on the bandstand and onto Big Sid, who lifted him high as Buddy grabbed both sides of Sid's head and planted a kiss on his forehead—*The Welded,* Ben Shahn could have titled this tableau, "Jazznocracy" personified, to use the actual title (no savant would risk it) of a 1934 recording by Jimmie Lunceford's black orches-tra. It was composed and arranged by a white man, Will Hudson, who worked mainly for the finest black bands of the twenties and thirties, a rarely mentioned tributary of jazz multiculturalism that was kept open and alive by Red Rodney's 1949–52 stint with Charlie Parker. When Parker and his otherwise black quintet toured the South, where racially mixed bands were not acceptable, he billed Rodney as "Albino Red, Blues Singer." He would sing one number, atrociously. Once, at a small club owned by a Jew, Rodney, who was Jewish (né Robert Rodney Chudnick), sang the blues in Yiddish, and no local yokel was any wiser, the JOU slipping under the enemy's radar.

Parker best compressed these interracial ideals in one "live" per-formance. Recorded on December 25, 1948, in New York, he plays "White Christmas," by Irving Berlin (born Israel Baline, in Russia), syncopating the opening measures to a rumba beat and later quoting "Jingle Bells"—*We Wish You a Merry Russian-Jewish Afro-Cuban All-American Christmas, Man,* reads the Hallmark card, the only one in stock under the "Miscellaneous Multicultural" rubric at the drugstore. Parker has raised Picasso's JOU as an international banner and tilted Brancusi's *King of Kings* crown at a very jaunty angle, the way Fats Waller would cast his derby in movies such as *Stormy Weather* (1943),

37. Henri Matisse, *Monsieur Loyal* (the circus director), from *Jazz,* 1947.

38. A. M. Cassandre, *Pathé Electrique,* poster, 1932.

when he was swinging into high gear, both eyes on the camera, totally self-aware and confident of his game.

Jazzmaniacs agree that 1939 is the *annus mirabilis* of the jazznocracy, though it's difficult to be lighthearted about it because 1939 saw the arrival of total war in Europe. Matisse, designing *Monsieur Loyal* for *Jazz* during the Nazi occupation, must have subconsciously associated this figure of the circus director with "the dictator" because it resulted in one of two scary white images that are uncharacteristic of *Jazz* (fig. 37). The other is *The Wolf,* a symbol of the Gestapo. Isn't this Mr. Death, or a young child's first view of a bald, singing albino? Chase it away! The following list of classic discs, all recorded in 1939, is an unprecedented crop, stockpile, and hedge against war doldrums: Coleman Hawkins's "Body and Soul"; Billie Holiday's "Yesterdays"; Sidney Bechet's "Summertime"; Fats Waller's "Squeeze Me"; Duke Ellington's "Braggin' in Brass"; Count Basie's "Lester Leaps In," "Dickie's Dream," and "Taxi War Dance," all featuring Lester Young; Benny Goodman's "Rose Room," featuring Charlie Christian; Johnny Hodges's "Dream Blues"; Frankie Newton's "The Blues My Baby Gave to Me"; Benny Carter's "More Than You Know"; Rex Stewart's "Finesse" and "Solid Old Man," both featuring Django Reinhardt; Muggsy Spanier's "Big Butter and Egg Man"; Jimmie Lunceford's "Uptown Blues," featuring Snooky Young; Bobby Hackett's "Embraceable You"; Lionel Hampton's "Sweethearts on Parade" and "I'm On My Way from You," respectively featuring Chu Berry and Henry "Red" Allen; and—to let the titles fly, like the notes in a fleet solo by Fats Waller—Erskine Hawkins's "Tuxedo Junction"; Earl Hines's "Rosetta"; Charlie Barnet's "Cherokee"; Artie Shaw's "The Carioca"; Bud Freeman's "The Eel"; Jack Jenney's "Star Dust"; and Harry James and Pete Johnson's "Boo-Woo," a Mondrian resource. All these records have stood the test of time, as they say, the way that A. M. Cassandre's stylized 1932 78-rpm shellac phonograph record had already evolved into a silvery, Léger-toned, technologically immortal compact disc, its scale and close proximity to the viewer symbolizing the importance of recorded music in the life of Mondrian, for one (fig. 38).

Mondrian arrived in New York from Europe in October 1940. Unnerved by the war, the dignified and cerebral seventy-year-old artist hadn't completed a canvas in two years. But unlike many émigré or refugee artists and writers, Mondrian and his friend Léger would thrive in America, owing in large part to their unusual, very un-European openness to everyday American life and popular culture. "The most colossal spectacle in the world," Léger had written after his first visit to New York in 1931. "Neither cinema nor photography nor reporting have been able to contain the astounding event that is New York seen at night from forty floors up. It resists all vulgarization. It keeps its freshness," and Léger could have been expressing the enthusiasm of Mondrian, who was equally exhilarated in 1941 by the glittering profusion along the Times Square/Broadway stem, "Madhattan" (an oft-repeated pun)—its yellow cabs; multinational military uniforms; crowded window displays, EVERYTHING MUST GO; huge smiles on billboards; flashing news, DIMAG GETS HIT SINGAPORE FALLS; neon-lit theater marquees; fluttering little flags; penny arcades with blinking lights; and, above all, jazz, which Mondrian had praised in print as early as 1927. He was especially energized in New York by his discovery of boogie-woogie—a primitive, blues-based music, rhythmic rather than melodic. He was soon jitterbugging at jazz clubs and working again, listening to the 78-rpm records of such Negro boogie-woogie pianists as Pine Top Smith, Speckled Red, Cow Cow Davenport, Jimmy Yancey, Meade "Lux" Lewis, Albert Ammons, and Pete Johnson. The latter two performed and recorded most successfully as a duet. Their 1941 RCA Victor album, *8 to the Bar,* subtitled *Two Piano Boogie Woogie for Dancing,* may well have been Mondrian's favorite, since he owned two copies, one album cover heavily reinforced on its spine with adhesive tape. The titles of Johnson and Ammons numbers such as "Barrel House Boogie," "Movin' the Boogie," and "Sixth Avenue Express" should suggest that blues-based "boogie" is rarely melancholic, which is one reason it enjoyed wide popularity at the time, and was enlisted in early 1941 to support the Selective Service Act in the Andrews Sisters' "Boogie-Woogie Bugle Boy," the story of a star big band trumpeter who resents being drafted ("a big bring-down") but soon gets with the army's program—rhythm ready to save the world, to paraphrase Louis Armstrong.

There are in fact no Armstrong or Waller discs in Mondrian's surviving collection, no doubt because he avoided melody and thus vocals. "Let's sit down, I hear a melody," he'd tell his dance partner when the "live" band switched from boogie-woogie to a standard song. Mondrian certainly had no use for comical singing that would have disturbed the already delicate and unlikely alchemical creative balance of barrelhouse jazz and ethereal Theosophy, Mondrian's system of Buddhist-like mystical belief—infinite reaches and deep calm formally "depicted" by the Alpine white, off-white, and faint gray Mondrian pigments that defy photomechanical reproduction. Only the grainy dull white of empty canvas seemed to render Mondrian's earthly fate in 1940.

To see Mondrian the artist come to life again, look at the sequence of four Mondrians here and then imagine him in action, as it were, finishing *Composition with Red* (fig. 39), the first one, in London, almost entirely drained of color in 1939 by the war. Now he's standing very still before his London easel in 1940, getting little done, especially after German bombs have fallen near his studio, on one occasion shattering the windows. Next, observed in his small New York studio in 1941–42, he's listening to boogie-woogie 78s as he completes unfinished paintings he's brought with him from Europe. Then he creates his first new picture in two years, the template superstructure he titles *New York City I* (fig. 40), electrifying it the following year in *Broadway Boogie Woogie* (fig. 41)—1940s incandescence, not 1950s fluorescence.

This composition, busy enough to be called a Johnson-Ammons duet or piano trio—they added Meade "Lux" Lewis on "Boogie Woogie Prayer" (1938)—is governed by eight horizontal and six vertical bands (and disc-bound hands) of primary color and force, running without interruption from one edge of the all-over composition to the other, equivalent to the unrelenting, hammering manner of boogie-woogie performances, which rarely begin or end with out-of-tempo introductions or cadenzas. Mondrian's basic geometry *is* boogie-woogie for the nonce, the left hand's "vertical" bass line ostinato (propulsive repeated figures) playing against the right hand's "horizontal" dotted eighth or sixteenth notes, heavy chords, simple riffs, tremolos, and choruses of percussive single notes, spaced variously, positing a stop-and-go-traffic neon-light time overview of Broadway and Times Square. Synesthesia rules, and the painting swings. Listen especially to its driving horizontal lines: *Yellow white yellow/blue yellow red/yellow yellow yellow yellow.* A tremolo! Did Mondrian ever dance alone in his studio?

Victory Boogie Woogie quickens the tempo and raises the volume (fig. 42), as though Mondrian were now listening to Pete Johnson's "Boo-Woo," "Cherry Red" (1940), and "Roll 'Em, Pete" (1938)—these 78s were all in the artist's collection—where Johnson is accompanied respectively by the trumpeters Harry James, Oran "Hot Lips" Page, and the blues shouter Joe Turner—no mere "vocalist"—who thunders "yes, yes, yes, yes!" percussively, Johnson playing unaccompanied pile-driver piano with such force that in person his piano would actually move. *Victory Boogie Woogie* raises a sea of flags, ready to celebrate V-J Day in August 1945, when thousands danced in Times Square and

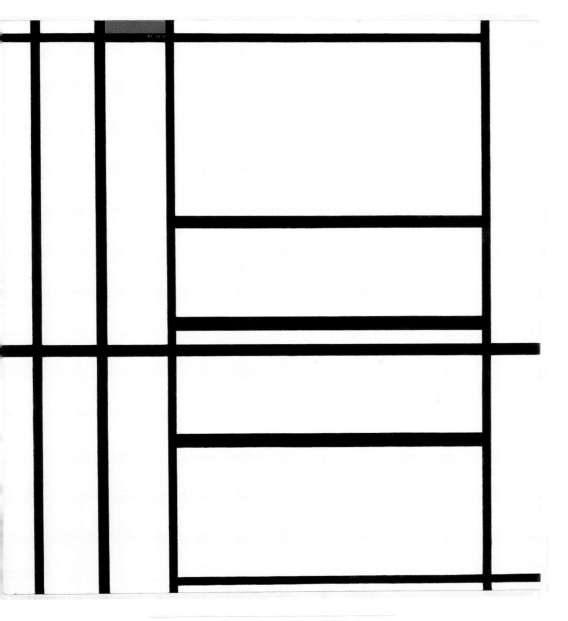

39. Piet Mondrian, *Composition with Red*, 1939.

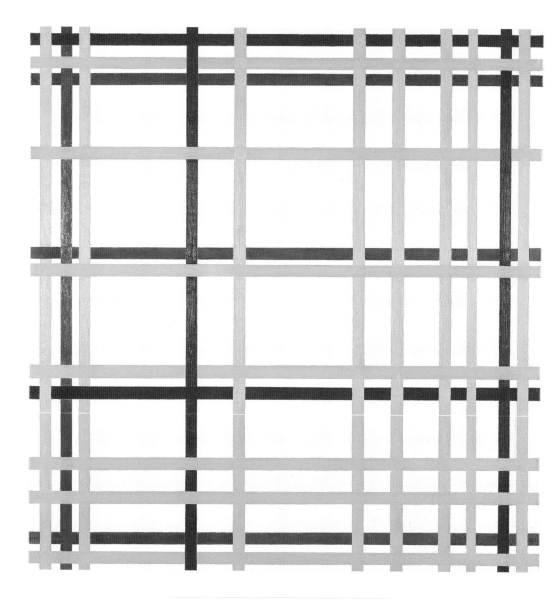

40. Piet Mondrian, *New York City I*, 1942.

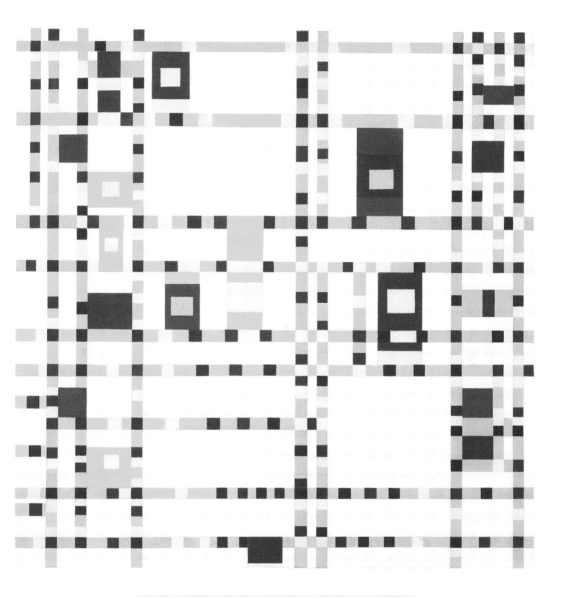

41. Piet Mondrian, *Broadway Boogie Woogie,* 1942–43.

42. Piet Mondrian, *Victory Boogie Woogie,* 1942–44.

VICTORY RED ....—A new lipstick

Elizabeth Arden
691 FIFTH AVENUE · NEW YORK

43. "Victory Red" lipstick, magazine advertisement, c. 1942–43.

44. "Diamonds Are Forever": until they move to Los Angeles. The 1941 Brooklyn Dodgers infield (left to right): Harry "Cookie" Lavagetto, Harold "Pee Wee" Reese, Billy Herman, and Dolph Camilli. The infield as a symbol of selfless team play was an attractive cliché of the day. Ernest Hemingway, a fan and sports symbolist, hung out with many of the Dodgers during 1941 spring training (see pitcher Kirby Higby's 1967 memoir, *The High Hard One*), including outfielder Pete Reiser, whose potential greatness was denied by numerous serious injuries, including the seven times he ran into unpadded outfield walls. A June 1947 collision left him paralyzed for ten days. A priest gave Reiser the Last Rites. He could have served Hemingway as a "code hero" like Joe DiMaggio in *The Old Man and the Sea* (1952)—at least one vision of Reiser preserved in literature.

along Broadway. To the Theosophist, the diamond-shaped image isn't finally a picture on a wall but a window or transparent ceiling, a visionary's glimpse of an infinite expanse of balance and order extending in every direction—a planetarium of the spirit. Screwball musical quotations launched by Charlie Parker are spotted in orbit through the Carl Hubbell telescope. "Diamonds are forever," in the familiar phrase that projects the essence of baseball nostalgia, an agreeably uncomplicated aspect of jazz modernism (fig. 44). "And rhythm saved Mondrian," Armstrong might have added, propounding *The Red Studio* solution (fig. 13)—the idea that art inspires art and much, much more.

Although many prominent New York artists and intellectuals signed pacifist petitions in 1942, refusing to aid the war effort, Mondrian knew that the London Blitz was not an abstract philosophical or political issue. *Victory Boogie Woogie* really follows the letter of the lightweight "Rhythm Saved the World." The 1936 Saul Chaplin–Sammy Cahn number celebrates rhythm's role in several major war victories through history. At "The Battle of Bunker Hill," sings Armstrong, the soldiers were tired until "drum and fife brought men to life." The same transpired in France in World War I until "the drummer struck up the band." Armstrong's band then quotes the *Marseillaise,* as does the trumpeter in his concluding solo—international notes as uncharacteristic of America's isolationist and willfully amnesiac 1930s as the patriotic chord in *Victory Boogie Woogie* is typical of the quotidian American culture, 1941–45, when even Duke Ellington turned a war propaganda slogan into song—"A Slip of the Lip (May Sink a Ship)" (1942)—and the V-word and signal letter appeared everywhere as the prefix to most anything, including "Victory Bonds"; "Victory Savings"; "Victory Gardens"; "Victory Red" (fig. 43); *Victory Cook Book; Victory Recipes; Victory Cakes* (a free pamphlet of sugar-saving recipes from Crisco); "Victory Hair Pin Kit"; "Victory Tonic"; *Victory Parade* (radio broadcasts of "live" big band performances); "Victory Society" (a comic-book club); "Victory Girls" (paper dolls in various uniforms); and "Victory Rummy" (playing cards that bore the faces of Hitler, Mussolini, and Tojo). The little *V* (for Victory) that was printed in the lower left- or right-hand corner of posters, magazine covers, and ads was often accompanied by the Morse code signal for *V,* three dots and a dash. Thanks to constant play on the radio, this onomatopoetic musical shorthand for the famous *allegro con brio* from Beethoven's Fifth was recognized by almost everyone—a high-class jingle, since there wasn't time to play a symphony. If the 1943 song "Victory Polka" was feasible (recorded by the Andrews Sisters), then a composition called *Victory Boogie Woogie* seemed quite natural. "Bad taste is . . . one of the valuable raw materials for the country [America]. Bad taste, strong colors—it is all here for the painter to organize and get the full use of its power," Léger said in 1945, on his return to France. He could have been discussing Mondrian's victories on several fronts, unaware of his secret weapon: Apollinaire's antenna/magnet on full power, its gauge set to receive "Victory, war; every slogan, product, ad, and title." By absorbing, transmuting, and telescoping this vast, kitschy "Victory" compost without embarrassment or irony, Mondrian the uncompromising abstract painter, theorist, and war refugee had joined the united front and jazznocracy, and even realized the ambitions of youthful scrap-collectors who, forming a literal tin-pan alley, could only imagine war-winning transmutations of their own salvaged stuff (figs. 45, 46).

If Mondrian had lived to witness the V-J Day spectacle in New York harbor—the day-long sounding of every whistle, bell, foghorn, siren, and claxon—he might have thought that his unfinished *Victory Boogie Woogie* had done justice to this grand rehearsal or aural rough draft of a *Victory Symphony* by Varèse, jazz modernism for *tout* Manhattan, with room for pot-banging by the scrap-collectors and boys in every neighborhood. *Baby Flat Top* (1946), by Mondrian's friend Calder, must have been conceived that day (fig. 50). The wire-limned trajectories of airplanes landing, circling, and taking off from the carrier are also a record of the sound levels in New York Harbor that day and Calder's own victory dance, quite intricate on the lower right.

Attempts by Mondrian and Robert Rauschenberg to evoke music afford an opportunity to anchor the definition of "Jazz Modernism." Abstraction notwithstanding, Mondrian's boogie titles make the pictures irrefutably "musical" and accessible, two examples of jazz modernism as perfect as Waller's transformation of "Jingle Bells" and Picasso's found, collaged depiction of happiness, *Guitar, Sheet Music, and Glass*. But Rauschenberg's "combine painting" (as he calls his assemblages) of the musical identity of Thelonious Monk, titled *Monk* (1955, fig. 48), is not jazz modernism because it doesn't swing or sing—that is, its collage doesn't make any verbal sense, one of the considerable achievements of the celebrated 1912–13 collages of Picasso, Braque, Sonia Delaunay, and the infinitely legible Carlo Carrà (fig. 98). Jazz and collage are literally one, finally, unless the serene sheet-music fragment in Picasso turns out to have been ragtime. Rauschenberg's collaged 78-rpm record label shard of Monk's most famous composition, "Round About Midnight" (1947), is a jagged fragment, a phrase that telescopes the essence of Monk as minimalist piano player and composer, especially his dissonances, like the nerve-racking way the lines of the trumpet and alto saxophone refuse to mesh in the ensemble passages of "Round About Midnight," enough to crack or shatter a 78 disc. Rauschenberg's tangled if not agonized Abstract Expressionist impasto pigments at the top of *Monk* are truly off-key, cacophonous rather than dissonant, viscerally wrenching like war carnage, a point reinforced all too well by the horrific "design" shared by Rauschenberg and the war photograph (fig. 49). At this juncture, *Monk* could reasonably be retitled *The Waste Land*—Picasso's BATAILLE badly decomposed.

Moving laterally, to the right, the fragment of pastoral landscape does capture Monk's lyrical and light side, particularly the pianist's halting and spare treatment of old-time songs and the big hits of other people. Monk challenges himself and amuses his listeners when he plays chaste, unaccompanied piano versions of songs associated only with the famous, high-gloss, circa-1941 big band collaborations of Tommy Dorsey and Frank Sinatra: "I'm Getting Sentimental Over You" (1957) and "Everything Happens to Me" (1959). Monk's musical surprises can be exhilarating, as when he shifts gears without warning, doubling the tempo and playing a chorus of mighty two-handed stride piano in the manner of James P. Johnson or Waller—a modernist acknowledging his roots and chosen route. "I'm Fats, slimmed down—starved! Less is more!" he is saying in effect whenever he juxtaposes robust piano voicings and spare ribs. But Monk's musical parodies and jokes aren't meant to kill. On "These Foolish Things" (1952), for instance, he quotes from "Please, Mr. Sun," pop singer Johnnie Ray's current hit—a foolish thing indeed, affording a droll contrast between pianist Monk's Pinter-like pauses and the hysterical manner of Ray, whose biggest hit was "Cry" (1951). Monk's parsing and editing of familiar songs make it clear that he, no less than Armstrong, wants to reveal and highlight the core of worthy sentiment in a sentimental song. The bloody pigments running down the pastoral in *Monk* are quite out of character for him. This "red weather" is bad enough to sicken the sailors on the flat-top USS *Wallace Stevens*—to posit a postwar navy governed by Eros.

Attempts to give visual form to Monk's idiosyncratic gifts beg obscurity. To project his considerable musical wit and humor, Rauschenberg offers a bottom-line film strip of Charlie Chaplin in *The Gold*

46. Victory Ragpickers Boogie, 1942. Boys of the Grand Street Settlement House on Manhattan's Lower East Side conduct a campaign to salvage aluminum that will be recycled as war weaponry—a conversion they seem to envision clearly in the poster Henry Koerner would paint for the U.S. Office of War Information in 1943 (fig. 45, opposite). The fellows in the foreground are driving the band, so many Jo Joneses making do with ad-hoc cymbals.

Rush (1925). It's the great scene when he stages a wondrous short dance on his humble dinner table, using two forks (legs) stuck into twin dinner-roll feet, the quirky rhythms and steps of the performance— pure genius—a conflation of balletic and eccentric vernacular turns that anticipate the brilliant eclectic styles of Fred Astaire, the Nicholas Brothers, and George Balanchine's 1930s choreography for Broadway and Hollywood. Chaplin's presence here connects Rauschenberg with the first generation of modernists who paid generous tribute to Chaplin, especially Hart Crane, E. E. Cummings, and Léger, who grants Chaplin sawtoothed Africanesque hair and Cubist angularities to suit the Little Tramp's optimistic bouncy step, which Léger syncopates wildly in his animated cartoon of Chaplin at the start and finish of his and Dudley Murphy's thirteen-minute film *Ballet mécanique* (1924), whose Chaplin images are based on Léger's illustrations for Yvan Goll's splendid 1920 *sui generis* "film poem," *The Chaplinade* (fig. 47). Few viewers, however, are likely to "get" Rauschenberg's Chaplin analogy. Does the other collaged stuff—a postage stamp, a piece of an air-mail envelope, two frames from the comic strip *Polly and Her Pals*—represent musical discontinuities in Monk, further dissonances? They vex, and are lost, like hermetic allusions in Joyce, Eliot, and Pound—and, by now, references to the Chinese poem "Please, Mr. Sun." In regard to collage, we were weaned on Picasso, who surgically improves JOURNAL as JOU—clear French for "game," but Rauschenberg's is a perverse one. He has eviscerated the record label's signal, mood-defining word "Midnight" and curiously veiled his attempt to communicate a sense of the most accessible aspect of Monk's often difficult music: its asymmetrical, stutter-step rhythms.

Monk's unique rhythms are achieved by the ways in which he and his drummer angle and space their notes and accents around and off the strong 4/4 beat of the bass player. Rauschenberg tries to transcribe this visually as the interplay between the field of bold, steady (bass line) dots and the eccentric, aysmmetrical beats of Chaplin's dancing rolls— which, like the Homeric subtext of *Ulysses,* are silent to begin with, barely discernible on the film strip, and beyond the comprehension of all save Talmudic or monkish close-readers. Given this situation, the dots loom large. Rauschenberg probably drew them from Stuart Davis's punning and percussive *Rapt at Rappaport's* (1952), the title a reference to a swinging New York toy store, "wrapped" and "rapped" fun, depending on the toy or game. Faced with Monk as a subject, the word- and jazz-oriented Davis might simply have included one or more of

Monk's waterbug dance titles: "Skippy" (1952); "Trinkle, Tinkle" (1952); "Off Minor" (1947); "Nutty" (1954); "Criss Cross" (1951); and "Rhythm-A-Ning." But Rauschenberg invokes no words and veils the dots, muting their effect, as though such overt expressiveness represents simple-minded enthusiasm on his part—Mondrian without the metaphysics—and that's definitely not hip. The title of Monk's "Let's Cool One" (1952) is operative. Postmodernism is around the corner for Rauschenberg, the new "king of the ragpickers" and Thanatos to the Eros of Armstrong, Waller, and Ellington. There's no place in the House of Rauschenberg for unembarrassed Picasso's flowering wallpaper of 1912 (fig. 8), though his no-frills *Woman in a Garden* would fit (fig. 9) and Apollinaire's antenna/magnet could prove useful, its powers tripled to pull in the heavy stuff savored by Rauschenberg—tatty beds, stuffed animals, big ventilation ducts.

Monk *was* cool, and unconcerned about accessibility. Can you hum such Monk masterpieces as "Criss Cross" or "Evidence" (1948), the rights of swing? It took twenty-five takes to record Monk's "Brilliant Corners" (1956), and the issued record is nonetheless a spliced-together piece. Some twenty years younger than Armstrong, Ellington, and Waller, Monk was never obliged to entertain or provide dance music. Maybe he's only a jazz modernist when he's recording recognizable old songs such as "Tea for Two" (1956) or "Just a Gigolo" (1958)—a great Armstrong number—or dancing by himself. Sometimes, when Monk's band was on a job and deep in his groove, he'd rise unexpectedly from the piano bench and do a stiff, lurching, almost spasmodic shuffle dance—an elbow shoots out at an angle, his other shoulder drops, he stops, he starts, he sways, Léger's Little Tramp in slow motion, Monk's feet marking off no more than two or three successive, overlapping, invisible squares. Back and forth he moves, in front of the piano, a choreographer and teacher by accident, unconsciously diagramming his complex rhythms in the air for the benefit of interested squares, members of the band, and off-duty musicians lining the bar.

To the right of Monk, John Coltrane, his eyes tightly shut, is soloing on the tenor saxophone. (It's October or November 1957, at the Five Spot, New York City, during Coltrane's six-month stint with Monk.) The sound of Monk's suede shoes slapping against the floorboards instead of any piano accompaniment must have "awakened" Coltrane, whose tumbling flow of phrases immediately gave way to conductor Monk's visible moves, transposed and voiced by the open-eyed Coltrane as ten or twelve staggered, single-note tenor keenings akin to Joe Turner's eleven "yeses" on "Roll 'Em, Pete" except that Coltrane's are rhythmically oblique stabs, in step with Monk, Coltrane's hard iron tone sharp enough to draw blood—Rauschenberg's *Monk,* after all, whose execution at least prefigures the musical modes of the avant-garde "free jazz" movement of the 1960s. Coltrane and Eric Dolphy, two of its leaders, would solo up-tempo for twenty or thirty varyingly eloquent and frenetic minutes, nonstop, their realization of Melville's assertion that an artist must be someone willing to say "No! In thunder." Retitled *Coltrane,* Rauschenberg's *Monk* becomes an epochal masterpiece.

This jazz new wave eschewed the salient characteristics of 1920–1950 classic jazz: accessibility; humor; a capacity for joy; the Great [white] American Songbook, the backbone of jazz multicultural-ism (music by Gershwin, Berlin, Rodgers, Cole Porter, Jerome Kern, Harold Arlen, Vincent Youmans, Hoagy Carmichael, Arthur Schwartz, Vernon Duke, Harry Warren); and the goals and ideals of racial integra-tion. "Jazznocracy"? A broken record, it seemed, raw material for a Rauschenberg collage—but free jazz didn't replace Armstrong et al., who held their ground in the sixties' victorious War Against Melody, that establishment stronghold. Jo Jones, who never played or recorded with Monk or Coltrane, is smiling stiffly in the wings. He's committed to help out here, and will, if asked; truth be told, however, he'd rather work his first aqua show—dancing whales, heavy-handed cymbalism to sustain the act.

47. Fernand Léger, *Charlie Chaplin*, 1924.

48. Robert Rauschenberg, *Monk*, 1955. "Combine" painting: oil, newspaper, fabric, printed reproductions, postage stamp, phonograph record, and wood on canvas. 14″ × 12″.

49. *His Battle Station* (original news service caption), c. 1944. Photograph by
PhoM1/c Arthur Green, U.S. Coast Guard.

OVERLEAF: 50. Alexander Calder, *Baby Flat Top,* 1946. Sheet metal, wire, and
paint.

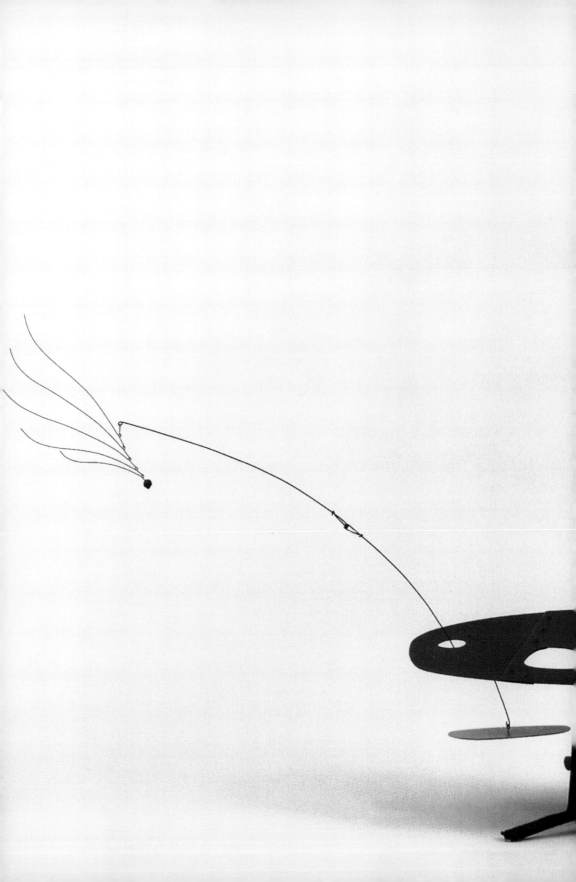

51. Alexander Calder, *Whale,* 1937. Sheet metal, bolts, and paint. 6′ high.

2

Kings of Razz

As extroverted singers who offered discursive material, Armstrong and Waller present striking, instructive contrasts. Armstrong the trouper usually did the best he could with silly, dubious, or offensive lyrics, though sometimes, like the Elizabethan clown, he used his persona of joy to take splendid liberties. "I'm a ding dong daddy from Dumas / And you oughta see me do my stuff," he sings in 1931. After warbling another silly line, he suddenly croaks: "Oh, uh, umm [sounds to that effect, verbal treading of water], and I done forgot the words!" This he confesses with more glee than guilt. Did his listeners understand that Armstrong was declaring the song dumb? Does this constitute cultural criticism of (white) Tin Pan Alley's hold on America? This surely can be said of Waller's singing, though it wasn't what he set out to do as a serious youngster devoted to the piano, classical as well as jazz.

Thomas "Fats" Waller—"Tom" or "Thomas" to his friends and family—had formidable technique, akin to a great athlete's, and, like Calder, an exhaustless inventiveness and capacity to delight. His articulation of notes was impeccable, however fast the tempo. His dramatic sense of dynamics allowed two-handed thunderstorms to give way suddenly to delicate raindrops struck by his right hand—to wax poetic quite overtly, a risk that Waller was willing to take whenever he played the pipe organ, from Bach (unrecorded) to "St. Louis Blues" to traditional Negro spirituals. The powerful oompah of Waller's left hand could serve alone as his rhythm section. At a time when live music was the rule, Waller the one-man band found steady employment in and around New York City from the age of sixteen, much to the chagrin of his very proper parents. If Waller had been independently wealthy or had a Lincoln Center appointment, he would have performed as an organ or piano soloist exclusively (for the latter, listen to "Handful of

Keys," "Numb Fumblin'," and "I've Got a Feeling I'm Falling," from 1929, all composed by Waller, who famously squandered his great gifts as a songwriter). To make a living, however, Waller drew on a comedic side further stimulated and loosened by the alcoholism that had set in by his mid-twenties. Waller's destiny as a jazz entertainer was determined by the successful 1932–34 run of his own radio show, *Fats Waller's Rhythm Club,* on WLW, a Cincinnati station that blanketed the Midwest. Although he had been recording since 1922, only now, in 1934, did RCA Victor launch Thomas Waller the "personality" and his newly formed sextet, His Rhythm, as a regular recording and performing group.

Waller would become, after Armstrong, the jazz musician best known and most loved by the population at large. From May 1934 until his sudden death in 1943 at the age of thirty-nine, Waller recorded a staggering 402 numbers for RCA (plus radio transcriptions), only twenty of them as a piano or organ soloist. During the same period Armstrong recorded 235 numbers, for Decca, the most commercial of the major labels. Decca never ran out of ideas, many of them poor, for variously teaming their contracted artists—e.g., Armstrong's ludicrous 1936–37 recordings with two Hawaiian groups, The Polynesians and Andy Iona and His Islanders, part of a Hawaii boom in tourism and popular culture. These are arguably the worst records Armstrong ever made, and interesting as such. When he takes a muted trumpet solo after singing the silly lyrics of "On a Little Bamboo Bridge," the clunky pan-Pacific beat and cloying descant of the Hawaiian steel guitars and ukulele prove incompatible with Armstrong's dulcet tone and flowing, pliable rhythm—Multicultural Hades, where there is no chance of saving a song. Even Fats Waller wouldn't have been able to overcome these guitars. Armstrong's plunge here locates exactly the problem faced by popular artists of talent: the dearth of first-rate songs. Benny Goodman, the only contemporary of Waller's who recorded more than he, employed the best arrangers to make truly poor dance numbers sound perfectly mediocre. Even if Waller could have summoned the discipline to write more songs as fine as his "Honeysuckle Rose," "Ain't Misbehavin'," "Keepin' Out of Mischief Now," "Jitterbug Waltz," and "Blue Turning Grey Over You," he still couldn't have come close to satisfying the demands placed upon him by his own success and the executives at RCA Victor.

Waller's band could readily produce great lyrical, instrumental recordings—"Blue Turning Grey Over You," for instance (1937), Gene

Sedric playing the alto sax sotto voce to please Debussy, it seems—but the RCA executives deemed vocals a commercial necessity. Their fiscal mindset is telescoped by the alternate takes of the oft-sung "I Can't Give You Anything but Love, Baby" (1939). The mediocrity of the first take, a comical vocal duet with the teenage Una Mae Carlisle, must have moved Waller to ask for a second take, without Carlisle, which is lifted by one of Waller's most inspired piano solos. The record producer opted for the first take—lyrics and laughs make the cash registers ring, which sounds like a business motto. In George Orwell's *Nineteen Eighty-four* (1949), a pop music machine cranks out rhymed songs nonstop— "for me," Waller might well have moaned. Atget's photo of the ragpicker (fig. 7) could pass as a Tin Pan Alley messenger carting in new sheet music for Waller and his band.

The demand for fresh material for Waller was largely filled by "novelty songs," as this musical fodder was charitably termed—a way of making light of weightlessness. Waller and his group would typically record six or eight new numbers every two months. Often he'd be seeing the music for the first time at the recording studio. A brilliant quick study, Waller would set up a number in fifteen minutes— inventing and humming riffs to his musicians, sequencing their solos, then reading the song's lyrics a second time through. There was rarely time for a rehearsal, and the reissued, alternate second takes of his records reveal that Waller the pianist never made a mistake. The record producers always had plenty of sandwiches and gin on hand, though sessions weren't necessarily a joy. Sometimes Waller would rail against a notably weak song, and storm around the studio shouting that he couldn't possibly record such junk. But he did. This Waller is a representative man, a fellow with a job to do. Whose job is always satisfying? But Waller could be inspired by the worst material, as though he had to live up to a motto or manifesto: Never Let a Sleeping Dog Tune Lie. To pun on the last word is to contemplate the subject of musical and verbal corruption and to pinpoint the challenge to Waller and, say, Artie Shaw, who couldn't stand it and quit early.

Waller takes on shallow songs with the surgical glee that Calder exhibited throughout the 1930s as he assayed and assaulted cartoonlike creatures of the sea/see who seem out of their depth or over their heads in gallery spaces that appear aquatic. If works such as *Form Against Yellow* (1936) had political titles—*Ethiopia,* say, evil white invades black (fig. 52)—viewers would see that Calder's jabs might be even sharper than Waller's, and not high Disney, as some have thought. The *Whale*

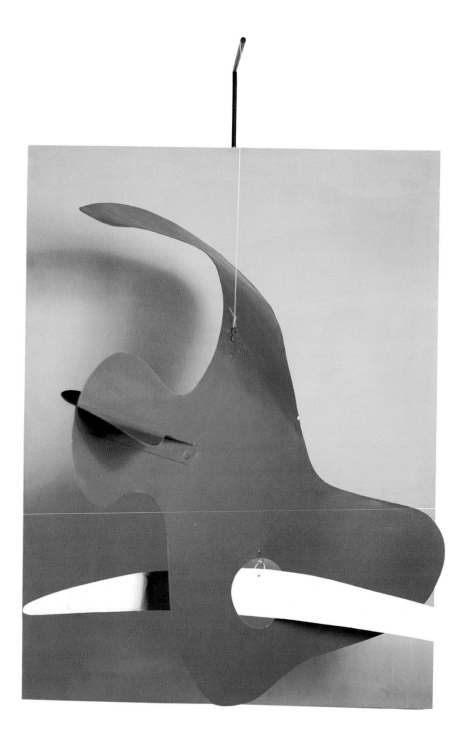

52. Alexander Calder, *Form Against Yellow,* 1936. Sheet metal, wire, plywood, string, and paint.

53. Alexander Calder, *Mobile,* c. 1934. Sheet metal, metal rods, and cord.

(1937) seems headed in that direction (fig. 51), but *Mobile* (circa 1934) is admirably balanced and tricky. Austere pieces pass muster as live, organic, undersea creatures whose open "fish mouths" can also be "read" as fin tails that address us directly (fig. 53): Are we coming or going? Which end is up? How deep is the ocean? Waller the musician negotiated these currents with absolute confidence.

Waller sends up and sometimes saves trivial and stupid songs by various means: sarcastic or falsetto delivery of some or all of the lyrics; mock-operatic singing, usually in the bass range; fulsome humming; heavy sighs; gospel-meeting exhortations; Bronx cheers; interjections in perfectly inflected Oxford or West Indian or Yiddish-American English; and a wide range of convincing sound effects. Waller's ad-libbed punch lines or verbal codas at the ends of songs are signature flourishes. "Git that basket fixed!" he cracks at the end of "A-Tisket, A-Tasket" (1938), a very silly novelty song made popular by Ella Fitzgerald. Waller's ad-libs can be both funny and sharp social commentary, as in his apostrophe to an otherwise pretty gal, "Your Feet's Too Big" (1939), when Waller adds, grandly, at the end, "Your pedal extremities are really obnoxious." His is the compensatory pomposity of insecure, self-inflating people everywhere, from preachers to police who have just "apprehended the alleged perpetrator." The high-falutin tag is mordant, too, if Waller intends to demonstrate that the shallow "lookist" he's playing, whose grammar is black vernacular—"I hates you 'cause your feet's too big"—also has the King's English at his disposal, so don't be so surprised. Had he lived, he could have had a major acting career—the black Zero Mostel and a lambent Falstaff. Waller was in truth well-read, and traveled with a volume of Shakespeare's plays. "One never knows, *do* one?" are the very last words of "Your Feet's Too Big," the *do* receiving heavy emphasis. Does you know why?

No African-American jazz entertainer of the 1930s escaped the call to record racist or racially dubious songs. Even the reserved and refined Negro bandleader Fletcher Henderson, a college graduate, recorded his own arrangement of "Underneath the Harlem Moon" (1932). Its opening choruses, before the band enters, consist of full-throttle solos by his star sidemen, Coleman Hawkins on tenor sax and Rex Stewart on cornet, as though their deep, manly voices—their figurative brass—would distract listeners from the ensemble's complicity and literal support of the song's demeaning lyrics, sung by Katherine Handy (W. C. Handy's daughter), which include, "They [Harlemites] just live on dancin' /

They never blue or forlorn / And it ain't no sin to guzzle down gin / Now that's just why darkies were born," the last line echoing the title of the song sung by Frank Munn in *George White's Scandals of 1931,* and also recorded by the estimable Mildred Bailey (1931). The saxophone and brass then double the tempo in the recording, as though trying to run away from the compromising lyrics. They can't, notwithstanding a lovely, full-bodied concluding coda by Hawkins, an Armstrong-like power play, which seems to plead, "Please let this wash away those stupid words and absolve us." Fats Waller kills such songs and their relatives. Witness "Mandy" (1934), an innocent in most everyone else's eyes and ears.

"This ticklin' is so terrific," Waller crows while playing "Mandy," his punning verb covering the way he attacks the ivories and Irving Berlin's song. Waller is surprisingly hard on the sweet little melody, with its banal or cute (a close critical call) rhyme scheme: "Mandy," "handy," "dandy." Waller trills "Lalala-lee-lo" quite sarcastically and scrambles the lyrics with an indescribable gurgling sound. "Mandy" was featured in a new Eddie Cantor movie, *Kid Millions,* and the recording aimed to capitalize on this. Waller's scornful attack is thus especially surprising and probably had to do with the fact that "Mandy" had premiered as a blackface minstrel number in the *Ziegfeld Follies* of 1919 and was now back with Cantor starring in blackface—too late in the game for this jive, Waller seems to be saying. Blackfaced Bing Crosby in *Dream House* (1932) should have been the end, with its telescopic title. But the movie *Kid Millions* is minstrelsy nostalgia—a period piece, set at the turn of the century and featuring a show-within-the-show, the film's big "Minstrel Night" number. "You know, you're lucky," Cantor says to his Negro servant while blacking up for the big "Minstrel Night" number. His cruel irony would seem to be answered on Waller's recording when trumpeter Herman Autrey uncharacteristically brays and whinnies like a donkey and a horse respectively—Spike Jones–like barnyard cacophony aimed at Eddie Cantor and Mandy's plantation and Miz Scarlett herself, shortly before her arrival. The enormous 1936 success of Margaret Mitchell's *Gone with the Wind* (the film appeared in 1939) only increased the call for Tin Pan Alley antebellum nostalgia, a staple product since Stephen Foster's day. Waller would wage uncivil war on any cotton corn that came his way.

Anti-bellum Waller is daring for its day, and still very funny because the objects of his parody—*Gone With the Wind,* of course, and the movie *Jezebel* (1938), and Foster and his progeny—are known to us still. Would that this were true of Joyce's sources in the "Oxen of the Sun" chapter of *Ulysses*. "Floatin' Down to Cotton Town" (1936) opens with the actual sounds of lapping, gurgling water and a steamboat's whistle, setting up the Foster-like genre scene that Waller then sinks with spirited playing by all hands and a burlesque of the question-and-response jokes of a traditional minstrel act. "Brother Bones, why does a chicken cross the street?" Waller asks and then answers himself: "They don't cross anymore. They stay over on my side." "Let's get away from here, let's get away," Waller says, dreamily, after the rambunctious music stops. The demise of "Old Plantation" (1937), its lyrics dripping with sentimental nostalgia, is hastened by Waller's comical mispronunciation of one word. "There's an old plantation in the *boot-eee*-ful South," he sings with deadpan sincerity after humming at the start in a mock-syrupy fashion. "Yes, there's an old cabin" he's really longing to see. "Yessss," he croons sonorously at the end (he had a fine voice), adding his own commanding coda, "Drop that plow," at which point the genre scene is suddenly drained of color (pun intended). In "My Window Faces the South" (1937), Waller croons that although he's far from the Swanee and it's "snowin' here," he's nonetheless "halfway to heaven" and "never frownin' " because he can still see "Fields of cotton smilin' at me / 'Cause my window faces the South." After his piano solo, he tells the band, "Come on, open the window," and the clarinetist obliges with a raw, rasping, window-opening solo. "That's it! Open *all* the windows," Waller yells as his trumpeter emits a strong, extroverted solo that's aimed in a Southern direction. "Let's get Southern atmosphere here," Waller says, the *get* serving as a forked, aggressive verb. "Toot it, son, toot it! Turn it on!" he yells, as though they were riding through Georgia with General Sherman and his torch-bearing troops. While rehearsing for his second movie, *King of Burlesque* (1935), in which he played an elevator man, Waller boldly insisted that his scripted "Yas-suhs" be replaced with "Yes, Sir." "I'm Shootin' High" was his one musical number here. Black beauty seems at stake in Matisse's *The Cowboy*, from *Jazz* (fig. 54).

Everything was fair game for color-blind Waller. "Yes, I love my baby but she don't love me" (repeat) Waller sings on "Fats Waller's Original E-Flat Blues" (1940, words and music by Waller, thus the title). "She give me some squirrel juice / She's got me runnin' up a tree, up a tree," he sings, moaning facetiously as he burlesques the blues and intones "up a tree" a third time, emphasizing a definite position and truth: gritty, funky black soul brothers and sisters can deliver "authentic" songs by rote just as easily as the tritest white writers and pseudo-folk performers in thrift-shop overalls. And race-based romanticism can be rot. "I'm the shook, the shake, the Sheik of Araby," Waller sings (1938), grinding the song's spurious desert exotica into so much camel feed. "The Sheik of Araby" is one of his infrequent big band recordings, a reminder of the unhappy annual tours of one-nighters in the hinterlands he and his group endured with an expanded orchestra of strangers; even now, some hardcore jazz purists reject all big band music as a contrived commodity, debased folk music—the Marxist line in the thirties. Waller was also wary of false consciousness. "Lord, there's one of those Georgian Arabians," he exclaims with feigned surprise as Assistant Sheik Herman Autrey starts his trumpet solo. "Mercy! But watch out for them camels!" Waller warns. At the conclusion of "Spring Cleaning (Getting Ready for Love)" (1936), Waller convincingly imitates a raucous old vacuum cleaner being revved up. The machine faces a daunting challenge if it hopes to suck in the bits and pieces of all the songs that Waller has decimated, and even a few camel droppings may just do it in. Why didn't an RCA publicist crown him the King of Razz?

Only Slim Gaillard's various groups and the five-man black jive combo known as the Spirits of Rhythm (featuring the wild vocalist Leo Watson) razzed more relentlessly than Waller. The Spirits were truly Walleresque in the way that their first-rate acoustic guitarist, Teddy Bunn, also a comic singer, could send forth a delicate, single-note solo out of the verbal stew of parody, as in their 1945 send-up of Irving Berlin's "Coquette," which they describe as "chicken croquette" and several other dishes. "I'll Be Ready When the Great Day Comes" (1933) is a gospel song, delivered straightforwardly, it seems, in the manner of the Mills Brothers. But when the Spirits repeat the pious title refrain five times they drop the final, fatal "comes" and Bunn substitutes a rich guitar chord instead—*carpe diem* before heaven, they're saying, a rejection of the religion and religiosity then at the heart of Negro life. Watson's concluding cadenza, hummed in falsetto, underscores the point. Their spirit of rejection can be aggressively serious. "Junk Man" (1934) is supposed to celebrate the Negro neighborhood's

OVERLEAF: 54. Henri Matisse, *The Cowboy*, from *Jazz*, 1947.

abject but "picturesque" junk dealer, with his woeful nag and colorful scrap wagon. "Boola-boola, boola-boola," croons Watson, turning the title figure into a Yale man—beyond condescension and sentimentality, ruling out local color. "Walkin' This Town" (1941) mocks the "my gal is gone" genre of blues and Tin Pan Alley's poetry of loss, too. As Bunn sings each uninspired, lachrymose, bluesy line, Watson rolls over it verbally with the solemnly intoned song title and lyric "Willow Weep for Me"—ten times, cutting down at least one tree in the forest of top-heavy metaphors. The group even twitted "I Got Rhythm." Their fast-paced 1934 recording ends abruptly, with a slow, out-of-tempo coda that is hummed sarcastically by the five Spirits: "La-la-la / La-la-la," as if to say, "Well, all right, okay, the lyrics worked this time, once, for a change." But Waller was never a cynic or nihilist.

As "literary" turns, Waller's caprices and parodies are implicitly moral acts of character, the domain of traditional satire. He respected the idea of a serious subject. The lyrics of "Christopher Columbus" (1936), a good swing instrumental, are so vacuous that Professor Waller must ad-lib a redeeming history lesson at the end, declaiming: "In the year 1492, Columbus sailed the ocean blue—that's what I think." No wonder so many writers have admired and loved Waller, including Hemingway, John O'Hara, Philip Larkin, and Eudora Welty, whose "Powerhouse," probably the best story about jazz, was written in 1939 (and published in 1941) after she had seen Waller perform a one-night stand with a ragtag big band in her hometown, Jackson, Mississippi. Her version of Waller turns out to be a multicultural Proteus and paragon long before the fact of any program or call for action. "Sheik! Sheik!" he is proclaimed by his men when he wraps a towel around his head. He looks "Asiatic, monkey, Jewish, Babylonian, Peruvian . . . African," and his band is named the Tasmanians. "A universal figure," as professors used to say. Bookish folks can't resist Waller's range of verbal masks and send-ups of self-pity and the rhetoric of romance such as "If It Isn't Love" (1934); "I'm Gonna Sit Right Down and Write Myself a Letter" (1935); "I Ain't Got Nobody" (1935); "Somebody Stole My Gal" (1936); "It's a Sin to Tell a Lie" (1936); "Your Feet's Too Big"; and "Until the Real Thing Comes Along" (1937). In the middle of his delivery of its insipid lyrics ("I'd move the earth for you") Waller demurs—"You want me to rob a bank? Well, I won't do it!"—thereby drawing limits for romantic hyperbole and dubious symbolic acts. "I—I—I—I ain't got nobody," sings Waller at the end of the plaintive song, the repetition of the first-person pronoun emphasizing "his" singular,

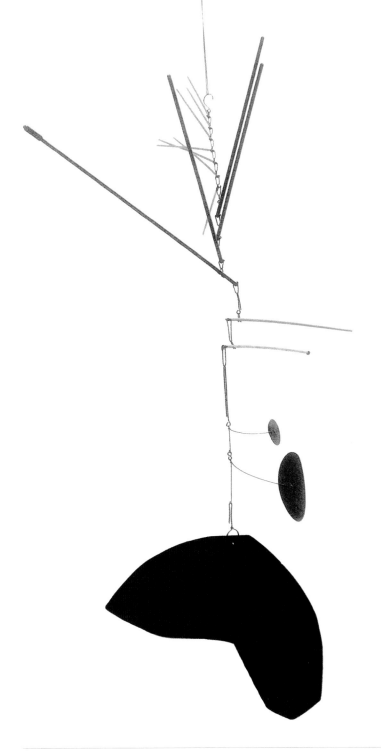

55. Alexander Calder, *Thirteen Spines,* 1940. Painted sheet metal, rod, and wire.

unsympathetic egotism. If you can't keep quiet, character will be outed—that's what I think. Such numbers are clearly not send-ups alone—hence their lasting appeal.

By today's standards, "Your Feet's Too Big" could also be called sexist, but Waller immediately manages to be humane as well as humorous, achieving the equipoise of art, however it's categorized and ranked. Waller opens the number alone at the piano, unaccompanied, treading gently. "Who's that walking around here?" he asks darkly, as the rhythm section enters. It's her feet, "baby elephant patter," he says, but the delicate tremolo he plays under these words says, in effect, big feet or not, she nonetheless moves with startling grace, like Calder's *Whale* or Oliver Hardy, doing one of his wondrously light soft-shoe routines in movies such as *The Music Box* (1932) and *Way Out West* (1937), or Jackie Gleason skipping with delight. "Somebody Stole My Gal" reverses this course as Waller withholds his affecting touch until the last instant. He delivers the song's sorry lyrics in a sobbing manner, with clownish "boo-hoos," but does manage to tell us he's sent detectives after the gal. "Quick, Sherlock, bring her back," he ad-libs at the end, "bring her right back on roller skates—*bring her! Bring her,*" he concludes in an altogether different voice. Waller has shifted gears unexpectedly with this repeated imploration, which sounds urgent and heartfelt, emoted as it is with the raw, piercing sincerity of a Jimmy Rushing, Count Basie's great blues and pop singer. The comedy isolates and heightens the poignancy of *bring her.* Parody, according to Proust, is a "cleansing, exorcising pastime."

There's no tonal lit'ry relief in "It's a Sin to Tell a Lie" because lying *is* bad, simply said. "I love you, I love you, I love you!" Waller declaims, with an insincerity unprecedented in the history of deceit and dissembling. Each "love" descends in pitch, from lying falsetto to lying basso profundo, punctuated by several hard, artificial laughs that sound like they're lies, too, drawn from comic-strip speech balloons: "HA! HA! HA!" "Get out there and tell your lie," he continues, a cynical command that could today be a rallying cry for contemporary minimalist writers to live up to the rich narrative potential of the lie, as in Conrad, Ford, Nabokov, and Welty's "Powerhouse." "What is it?" (your lie), Waller addresses his audience, and, surprisingly, the band answers with compelling clarinet and trumpet improvisations, totally praiseworthy nonverbal "lies," vaporizing the cynicism in the air. Waller casts a wide net, as does Calder. His reputation for programmatic gaiety (the *Whale*) is belied by the epochal *Thirteen Spines* (1940), whose skeletal remains and dead or dying whale stand for the reality of total war in Europe (fig. 55).

The meaning and emotional force of "Powerhouse" turn on two big lies, involving imaginary characters: a fellow named Uranus Knockwood, possibly one of the Devil's agents, and Gypsy, Powerhouse's wife—each a projection of Powerhouse's anxieties ("heebie-jeebies," in black folk parlance), his loneliness and depression, even. If you listen to forty or so Waller numbers in a row on one of the reissue CD sets, you'll feel exhausted, imagining an hour and a half on the job. You want to hand him a towel and tall glass of something. Surely one intermission isn't going to suffice! How can he keep this up? The unsettling bleakness of his vocal-free versions of the old spirituals "Deep River" (1938) and his very last recording, "Sometimes I Feel Like a Motherless Child" (1943), both recorded on pipe organ, suggests that he couldn't, or managed barely, and proffers a Pagliacci-like Waller perceived by Eudora Welty alone. "I wonder what the poor people are doing. I'd love to be doin' it with them," Waller says unexpectedly during his dirgelike "Motherless Child" solo, a recycled old "ad-lib" that here effects an inappropriate, unfunny, and jarring break in tone and mood—compulsive "humor" that would dispel or ease putative despair?

In the story, Powerhouse's joyous improvisations and manic exuberance give way to something else late at night. Groaning, he says, "You know what happened to me?" Valentine, the bassist, only hums a response. "I got a telegram my wife is dead," Powerhouse says. "Telegram say—here the words—'Your wife is dead.'" While he plays the piano he moans, "What the hell was she up to?" and shudders, "Tell me, tell me, tell me" (an imploration used by Waller in several recordings). Something from within finally "tells" him, and Powerhouse weaves a (tall) tale that blames Uranus Knockwood for Gypsy's death. It is improvised in tandem with his solo, his fingers "dragging the keys heavily." "What you tell me the name of this place?" Powerhouse asks Valentine, whose name signals the kind of message Powerhouse really needs to receive in place of vagrant "gypsy" love. "White dance, week night, raining, Alligator, Mississippi, long ways from home," answers prose-poet Valentine, who might have included complaints about the dance band, and the stock arrangements played by those anonymous section men all wearing eyeglasses—so they can read those arrangements rather than improvise. Welty didn't know how reluctantly Waller went on the road with a big band, but she somehow sensed this truth.

During the intermission, Powerhouse and three sidekicks, the nucleus of his regular group—"the real ones," Welty calls them—visit the ramshackle World Café in Negro-town (as it's called). Here he works a kind of black magic and seems to exorcise Uranus Knockwood and Gypsy from their midst and his very being. Gypsy, his "juju" or fetish figure, must die in the process, horribly—a suicide who jumps out a window because, according to Powerhouse, she misses him so horribly. Welty, a master of vernacular illusions and allusion, uses the titles of famous songs (no lyrics are quoted) to telegraph Powerhouse's state of mind and resulting behavior. They were playing "Pagan Love Song" when he started on Gypsy and now, in the World Café, he regally requests the juke box to play "Empty Bed Blues," followed by "Sent for You Yesterday and Here You Come Today," a blues sung by Jimmy Rushing with the orchestra of Count Basie, Waller's star disciple. The songs are as connotative and accessible as Hemingway's shorthand baseball references to the New York Giants' long-term manager John McGraw in *In Our Time*'s "The Three-Day Blow" (1925)—the baseball patriarch as opposed to the troubled fathers in the story—and Joe DiMaggio recollected in *The Old Man and the Sea* (1952) as the wounded warrior who carried his team. Baseball, like big bands then, was ideally a matter of team performance, which is why many swing fans knew the personnel of bands the way baseball nuts knew the names of every position player in the game. The most memorable chapter of Artie Shaw's autobiography, *The Trouble with Cinderella* (1952), relates the tireless way Shaw rehearsed his four-man saxophone section—his infield—apart from the orchestra. Many swing bands fielded a baseball team. Harry James, who recorded "Dodgers Fan Dance" (1941), was said to care as much about a band recruit's baseball skills as his musicianship. "Did You See Jackie Robinson Hit That Ball?" was Basie's only pop hit (1947).

The general course of Powerhouse's catharsis (if that's the word) is telescoped by Basie's superb recording of "Sent for You Yesterday and Here You Come Today" (1938), a five-step recovery program wherein the band responds to Rushing's piercing laments by expressing pain (the growly, rasping brass section, and Herschel Evans's moaning tenor saxophone solo); commiseration (trumpeter Buck Clayton's muted obbligato as Rushing sings, "Don't the moon look lonesome shining through the trees?"); and grit (Harry Edison's open-horn trumpet solo, legato but very firm). The last phrase of Edison's solo leads into and is absorbed by the band's aggressive, gleeful closing riffs—rolling, medium-tempo calls and responses between the brass and saxophones that, in a familiar phrase, blow the blues away, Jo Jones riding them out of town like a jockey on the home stretch, his drumsticks whirling freely around the basic 4/4 pulse, whacking the riff on each side as they head for a photo finish, the jitterbugs kicking up their heels. A few closing, relaxed piano notes sound, out of tempo—a musical sigh of relief as the ensemble relaxes. "The moon shines through the trees," at least one male dancer must have whispered to his partner.

Renewed, Powerhouse returns to the dance hall through a symbolic rainfall that is consistent with Welty's use of aquatic imagery through-out the story and indigenous to the region. "Mississippi River's here," says the waitress in the World Café of the heavy rain, a blue-note sounded throughout the story, as in countless blues, most strikingly Bessie Smith's "Back Water Blues" (1927), a product of the flood of that year, which drowned thousands of people. Powerhouse's head "rolls and sinks" while he plays "Pagan Love Song" and, earlier, deep in a song, he yells "like somebody in a whirlpool." In the World Café, he is introduced to the local hero, a huge, inarticulate Negro with "bursting eyes": "This here is Sugar-Stick Thompson, that dove down to the bot-tom of July Creek and pulled up all those drownded white people fall out of a boat. Last summer, pulled up fourteen." Powerhouse will not drown.

Back in the dance hall after intermission, Powerhouse "took hold of the piano, as if he saw it for the first time in his life, and tested it for strength, hit it down in the bass, played an octave with his elbow, lifted the top, looked inside, and leaned against it with all his might. He sat down and played it for a few minutes with outrageous force and got it under his power," writes Welty, rendering the audience's collective view of Powerhouse. But "who could remember any of the things he says? They are just inspired remarks that roll out of his mouth like smoke," she adds. He may be a creative dynamo, but he's ephemeral to them—a caricature or grotesque with no life of his own, certainly. He's still what he was at the outset of the story, when the audience took in his "long yellow-sectioned strong big fingers, at rest about the size of bananas"— Waller drawn and quartered by a thirties artist such as Miguel Covarru-bias. Only the reader knows about Gypsy and Uranus Knockwood. At the end of the story, Powerhouse is singing and playing "Somebody Loves Me," piling up twelve or fourteen choruses. His mouth, the

source of those smokelike remarks, "gets to be nothing but a vol-
cano"—the orifice of a cartooned Negro, a hot jazzman and holy-roller
preacher in one, as seen by an insensitive if not racist Southern audience.
Waller and Armstrong do in fact appear together as cartoon angels in
the animated film *Clean Pastures* (1937), a good-natured parody of the
1936 movie version of *Green Pastures,* Marc Connelly's once-famous
1930 Pulitzer Prize–winning play, a heaven-based fantasy with an all-
colored cast. However stereotypical and condescending it looks today,
with its great cotton-candy spun clouds (wind machines keep them
moving), *Green Pastures* does mark the central importance of the church
and biblical literalism in segregated but stable African-American com-
munities.

Waller, like Armstrong, frequently turns to the church for comedy
and genuine sentiment. Where Armstrong preferred production numbers with choirs—"Shadrack" (1938) and "Elder Eatmore's Sermon on
Generosity" (1938)—Waller favored discrete outbursts of churchly fervor. "Rock, church rock," he says quietly after Herman Autrey's muted,
surprisingly moving trumpet solos on "Sweetie Pie" (1934) and
Waller's own "B-Flat Blues" (1940 radio transcription), adding, imp-
ishly, on the latter, "I wouldn't be nothin' but a Baptist to save me."
"Everybody latch on!" Waller calls out when the band begins to riff on
the self-pitying "I Ain't Got Nobody"—music as transport. "Mercy!"
Waller exclaims on countless numbers, his most "literary" locution
because he intones the gospel tag so variously, registering ecstasy, or
prayer, or comedy, or all three at once, as at the end of "Swingin' Them
Jingle Bells" and the explosive "Dinah" (1935)—one of the best examples of the extraordinary power this small group could generate.
Waller's "Mercys" at once tweak unsophisticated religiosity and assert
that music-making is an act of faith.

Unlike Waller, whose father was a minister, nothing tempered
Armstrong's approach to the sanctified church. His recordings of "The
Lonesome Road" (1931) and Stephen Foster's "The Old Folks at
Home" (1937, made with the Mills Brothers) respectively offer light-
and dark-toned extremes. Foster's song is the lament of an "emanci-
pated" Negro who sadly roams the world, longing to return to the
plantation: "Oh, darkies, how my heart grows weary." Faced with these
repellent old lyrics, Armstrong dons the mask of Baptist deacon and
sends up the song with a "church service" cast in bitterly caricatured
and accented dialect, spoken after the crooning brothers have presented it straightforwardly: "That's where *my* heart is turning, river!"

says Armstrong, interpolating the Swanee. *"Yowsuh!"* he exclaims broadly. "Know one thing? My heart am still *longin'* for the old plantation—sing, brothers," and they do, heartily. "Hallelujah, hallelujah . . . Oh, darkies," Armstrong intones. "Look-a here, we're far from home. *Yeah!*" he exults at the end, sounding like Waller. The Dixie diaspora had its charms, but comedy had better be a musician's religion if old plantation/Swanee River songs were forced upon him by record company executives because they sold well, to black buyers, too. "It ain't over till the fat man sinks," a weary Waller might have punned, partaking of "Powerhouse's" most doleful aquatic imagery. Calder's waters contain their own July Creek miracle, the winning retrieval of a water-logged branch or piece of driftwood that is losing its battle with ramming, mighty carved wood—Calder's *Shark and Whale* of 1933 (fig. 56). "Praise the Log!" cries a spectral Waller from his *Clean Pastures* pulpit.

In "The Lonesome Road," a pseudo-spiritual in which he directs an almost anarchic verbal vaudeville at the expense of "his" down-home ministry, Armstrong plays a money-hungry preacher, the band his voluble congregation. While Reverend Armstrong makes the weekly collection, to meager results, he moans, "What kind of a church is this, what kind of church?" "Two dollars more would have got my shoes out of pawn," he whines, "but nevertheless I'm in love with you." This sort of patter has long been criticized for perpetuating caricatured Negro "types," though "types" sometimes do capture truths, a troublesome truth to consider, then or now. But Armstrong's reverend is dead-on and deathless satire if you forget race and only remember the TV evangelists of the 1980s. Armstrong's "I'm in love with you"—instead of "God loves you" or "I love you"—is a brilliant modulation, Jim and Tammy Faye Bakker before the fact. "Editor" Armstrong jettisons the shallow "sacred" lyrics of "The Lonesome Road" in favor of his own ad-lib ensemble clowning and over-the-top humming by the reverend's "choir," and his trumpet solo is the only dignified voice in the proceedings. Armstrong's burlesque of preachers was so brilliant that by the conclusion of a similar number in a Chicago theater, performed wearing a cutaway coat and battered top hat, his audience's response to his mock-Baptist calls grew so frantic that a woman "rushed down the aisle shouting, 'Don't stop, Brother Louis, don't stop.' The audience . . . broke up," recalls cornetist Rex Stewart in his memoir, *Jazz Masters of the Thirties* (1972). Eudora Welty renders such audience dynamics splendidly.

The great power and originality of "Powerhouse" is predicated on Eudora Welty's conflation of church and state—the state of a jazz musician who formulates the author's extraordinary sense of the tone and pace of a sanctified church meeting and the closed-off Negro world of "juju," of fear and deathly superstition. (Welty's assignments as a government documentary photographer gave her access to places normally off-limits to genteel Southern ladies in the 1930s.) Powerhouse enthralls everyone at the crowded World Café with his incredible tale of Gypsy, who has just committed suicide: "*Sssst! Plooey!* What she do? Jump out and bust her brains all over the world," he shouts. "Brains and insides everywhere, Lord, Lord," he chants—voodoo therapy performed with a fetish-effigy, a pagan love song indeed. But Powerhouse is manifestly a Baptist preacher (Welty actually didn't know about Waller's father) leading his ad-hoc café "congregation." The fast, syncopated call-and-response dialogue is sanctified church jazz, bound to chase the blues and most devils as well. Welty's got rhythm to spare, it turns out. The following passage should be read aloud, doing different voices extravagantly, the tempo doubled in the last five lines as the exorcism concludes:

> "Ya! Ha! You talking about . . . old Uranus Knockwood," says Powerhouse, "look down and say Jesus! He say, Look here what I'm walking round in!"

OPPOSITE: 56. Alexander Calder, *Shark and Whale*, 1933. Various woods. 34¼" high. The shape of this whale complements the penetrating (evil?) white "tusk" in *Form Against Yellow* (fig. 52), here a welcome sighting: the hunted gentle behemoth, often sentimentalized, shows its proverbial teeth. Indeed, this whale/tusk visual pun evokes monumental incisors ranging from prehistoric mammoths in museums to scarred old walruses. Calder knows that head-butting is a basic whale attack mode, though his aquatic creatures rarely bare their teeth literally. "I'm essentially a happy man," as Calder once told an interviewer who was pressing him about the way his work seemed to run uniquely against the currents of modernism, wrongly characterized once again as totally dark, joyless, and pessimistic—a half-truth. As it happens, the Calder Estate has just discovered that *Whale* (fig. 51) should in fact be titled *Devilfish*—the name of the manta ray and an American species of octopus. This turns whimsy into nightmare. One never knows, *do* one?

They all burst into halloos of laughter. Powerhouse's face looks like a big hot iron stove.

"Why, he picks her up and carries her off!" he says.

"Ya! Ha!"

"Carries her *back* around the corner . . ."

"Oh, Powerhouse!"

"You know him."

"Uranus Knockwood!"

"Yeahhh!"

"He take our wives when we gone!"

"He come in when we goes out!"

"Uh-huh!"

"He go out when we comes in!"

"Yeahhh!"

"He standing behind the door!"

"Old Uranus Knockwood."

"You know him."

"Middle-size man."

"Wears a hat."

"That's him."

Everybody in the room moans with pleasure. The little boy in the fine silver hat opens a paper and divides out a jelly roll among his followers.

The moan denotes release, relief—a collective catharsis. Everything is quite still for a moment, like many mobiles in the sea of Calder, who was always ready to riff on fish, however slim the pickings—e.g., his "shark" branch (fig. 56). Abstract, invisible evil has been given a name and height in the World Café and almost reduced to hat size. "Rhythm Saved the World" is once again the Armstrong title that best summarizes the proceedings.

If music-making is an act of faith, then Waller and Armstrong are bishops in the Church of Lost Songs, where it is truly Christian to save a dog tune. "You're Not the Only Oyster in the Stew" (1934) is one of the most inspiring Waller rescue operations, an encore suitable for Powerhouse. (The title toys, of course, with the verbal saw, "There are other fish in the sea.") Waller sings the song charmingly: "There's seven million people in New York / There's fifty million Frenchmen in Pa-a-ree / Not to mention such / As English, Irish, Italians, and Dutch / But you're the only one for me," he sings. He then swings into his piano solo with uncommon speed, to compensate for the inept scansion. Instead of allowing his right hand to skate off alone, to improvise and outdistance the tune, as in the "Jingle Bells" mission, Waller sticks to the melody and improves it with strong chording, dignifying the song's story line. The same thing happens in "Two Sleepy People" (1938) and "My Very Good Friend the Milkman" (1935), a potentially sentimental but credible and affecting direct-address proposal of marriage, à la Armstrong in its disarming sincerity. Waller's concluding ad-lib on "You're Not the Only Oyster in the Stew" is for once straight, addressed directly to the oyster herself: "Look out, babe, you're not the only oyster in the stew," which is to say, you really are. "Oh, babe, mercy," he had said earlier, earnestly interrupting the lyrics. We've been waiting for Waller to undermine the song completely—there have been one or two hints—but it turns out to be a plaint, presented seriously all along as a rejected or dejected lover's rationale and plea. The slightest note of sarcasm or musical burlesque would kill the emotion, and the number, as though one of the perfectly balanced component parts of Picasso's *Guitar, Sheet Music, and Glass* were tilted at a discordant angle (fig. 8). The Oyster Stew doggerel is good enough for the poor guy in the song—"water," according to fact and adage, "seeks its own level." The oyster is a pearl and so is Waller's performance. Calder might well have constructed a monumental oyster of steel to go with his *Red Petals* (1942), since it's a virtual Waller number—a circus seal spouting as well as sprouting blossoms (fig. 57). "Let the band play 'Here Comes the Bride,' " Waller ad-libs sweetly at the end of "My Very Good Friend the Milkman," without a wink or grimace, it seems. "Good night," he says simply at the end of "Two Sleepy People" after delivering its concluding line, "Two sleepy people, much too much in love to say good night." His good wishes are triply sweet and affecting in view of our expectations, especially if one knows the initial recording of this Frank Loesser–Hoagy Carmichael tune, a duet sung by Bob Hope and Shirley Ross, from their movie *Thanks for the Memory* (1938). They are suggestive and flip where Waller is tender and sincere—the heart of Hoagy, who readily wears his on his sleeve as a world-weary barroom pianist-singer who's invariably in (open-heart?) shirtsleeves in some ten movies (e.g., *The Best Years of Our Lives,* 1946), good public relations for self-consumed jazz musicians.

"Oh, mercy, banish every care," pleads Waller near the end of another 1930s performance. He and Armstrong make you believe they

wish this for each of us, as they did for one another; Armstrong cried all
night after he learned of Waller's sudden death. "Thomas! Thomas!" he
sobbed, according to trombonist Henderson Chambers. In the coda to
"Sweet Sue" (1935), paramedic Waller begs for "One more beat! One
more beat," and on some numbers it does kick in, as in Waller's last-
minute rescue of his shaken-up big band version of "The Sheik of
Araby," recorded by a touring ensemble hastily organized by Waller's
new manager to get him out of debt. After a bland trombone solo and
his customary Tom foolery, the orchestral Waller assumes full command and swings the underrehearsed ad-hoc ensemble from the piano,
their closing riffs surging and swelling with the medium-tempo tidal
force of Basie, drummer Slick Jones (no relation to Jo) inspiring the jitterbugs and whipping the loping camel to a hard-earned victory—over
the silly song, and Waller's antipathy to big bands, victory sweetened
by the fact that several of the underdeveloped black and blue forms in
Matisse's *The Knife Thrower* have started to dance (fig. 58). For once,
Thomas Waller doesn't let Fats ad-lib at the very end. Music has the
last word, so to speak; Matisse's two performers are mouth-free, silent,
as Jo Jones plays a long, circus-style drumroll in the wings.

OPPOSITE: 57. Alexander Calder, *Red Petals,* 1942. Wire, sheet metal, and
paint. 8′6″ high. Seals offer vernacular symbolism to the extent of one's knowledge of their amphibious survival skills, sonarlike perception, and extraordinary
stamina and agility—hence the U.S. Navy's Special Forces SEALS acronym. Seals
emit musical sounds while copulating, and nurse their offspring on shore for several months in crowded, very sociable colonies. The creature has been justly
anthropomorphized in lore and popular culture. The walrus, a relative, can almost
stand—tusks catching the light, one hopes.

OVERLEAF: 58. Henri Matisse, *The Knife Thrower,* from *Jazz,* 1947.

3

Pops Art

Armstrong's trumpet always has the last, saving "word" in the wake of any vocal that could be deemed unmanly in his effort to ingratiate himself to an audience and/or disguise a poor song. This is typically true of his 1930 recording of "Sweethearts on Parade," which ties with "Just a Gigolo" as Armstrong's bravest rescue operation—a perverse distinction that underscores his method. The choice is difficult, since sincerity of delivery rather than Walleresque satire was Armstrong's natural bent, and there are numerous beneficiaries. "Sweethearts on Parade" qualifies because of the giddy illogic of its simple lyrics by Carmen Lombardo. Armstrong sings, "Oh, two by two / They go marching through / The sweethearts on parade," imagining couples in their Saturday night finery struttin' their stuff on Beale Street. He continues, mournfully, "I'd love to join their fun / But they bar me, babe, uh / It takes more than one / To join their army." Why? Is it so gauche to appear without a date? Couldn't he hook up with one at the last minute? And can't a well-dressed, well-behaved man promenade alone? Why not? Because the song was written to be sung by a woman!

"Sweethearts on Parade" was first recorded in 1928 by an inferior singer named Lillie Delk Christian, accompanied by Armstrong, who quite rightly plays the blues for her; the verse, discarded in Armstrong's version, begins "All alone I stand / Looking out my window" at the army of sweethearts. Released under her name, this recording remains little known. But the lyrics now make sense: an attractive young woman parading alone could only be perceived as a prostitute. Armstrong the thespian projects enough heart-on-the-sleeve male misery for us to assume that he's immobilized by some recent, unremarked heartbreak. "Oh, love," he mumbles, swallowing the indigestible word after he completes the lyrics. He adds, stretching the line, *"Oh, the sweethearts . . . on . . . puh-ra-a-de,"* singing the seven syllables as the same note, recomposing and deconstructing the humiliating song, the new melody leading logically into Armstrong's purely instrumental variations—a strong, implicitly optimistic statement given the technical assurance of his playing, the kind of recovery we all can identify with and covet, and it's the root of his enduring appeal and popularity. *How to Transcend the Stupid in Everyday Life and Song* is the self-help book Armstrong and Waller could have coauthored, two "kings of the ragpickers." Trumpeter Armstrong executes three difficult stop-time breaks with ease, his tone remaining warm and full, and concludes his solo by quoting the famous opening trumpet break from the up-tempo jazz warhorse "Bugle Call Rag."

Armstrong plays the ascending "Bugle" runs in a surprisingly elegant, languorous manner—retarding, winding down the tempo at the end, a telling anticlimax that divests the quotation of its jazz aura. "Assembly," it's called, the traditional military bugle call to gather the troops for a parade, drill, or inspection, which Armstrong has just passed, progressing on this record from wimp to prodigious trumpeter, a veritable one-man army. His attack on "Sweethearts on Parade" projects what his basic musical procedures would be for years to come (1930–47) as featured performer with large ensembles: open with trumpet solo, one chorus (muted if a ballad), keeping the melody recognizable; follow with vocal; conclude with virtuosic open horn

---

OPPOSITE: 60. Charles Peterson took this photograph of Benny Goodman performing with his band at New York's Roosevelt Hotel in April 1935, several months before their nationally broadcast triumph at the Palomar Ballroom, Los Angeles, ushered in the Swing Era on August 21, 1935. The audiences at the Roosevelt, home base of Guy Lombardo—"The Sweetest Music This Side of Heaven"—recoiled from Goodman's glass-rattling, up-tempo numbers. The engagement "was a horror, a horror!" remembers the lead alto saxophonist, Hymie Schertzer. The band was quickly given two weeks' notice, which makes this photo an extraordinary document. For once, Goodman isn't wearing his familiar eyeglasses. Were they fogged up hopelessly by one of his hot solos or by sustained jazz ecstasy? How could this man not succeed? *"I'm gone,"* uplifted swing and bebop fans used to say.

improvisation (two choruses, rarely more), whose arclike structure calls to mind an operatic aria. Armstrong was in fact a devotee of Caruso and the Irish tenor John McCormack, Joyce's favorite—not to miss a chance to remove the fences or walls between "high" and "low" culture, which Léger and Calder accomplished smoothly, as in the former's *Accordion* (fig. 5).

Armstrong's 1930s tack established the basic procedure for swing bands dominated by one instrumentalist—Artie Shaw, Roy Eldridge with Gene Krupa's Orchestra, Charlie Barnet, Bunny Berigan, Benny Carter, Jimmy Dorsey, and Harry James. Although he lacked "personality," Benny Goodman best mastered the Armstrong big band formula by dint of his playing, his supreme confidence that his climactic clarinet solos could rescue prom-oriented "novelty" numbers burdened by silly lyrics: "Yankee Doodle Never Went to Town" (1935) and "Eeny Meeny Miney Mo" (1936). If Goodman's vocalists of the thirties, Helen Ward and Martha Tilton, had been jazz singers instead of big band vocalists—strict constructionists, always true to the tune—they might have slanted or scatted their delivery in a way that would have taken some of the pressure off Goodman, who tried to toot a weak song away, making us forget its lyrics immediately, the way Fletcher Henderson's soloists eclipsed "Underneath the Harlem Moon."

What *is* a jazz singer anyway? The question continues to vex jazz critics and enthusiasts. A simple answer: a jazz singer takes liberties with a song's melody, harmony, rhythm, and lyrics. The jazz singer's phrasing is like an instrumentalist's. For instance, the title lyric and additional lines in Armstrong's "You Are My Lucky Star" (1935) are so dim that only his vowel variations—"you," "yoooo," "yoo-uh," "yuh"—vivify the object of the worn metaphor. Fauvist Derain's singular attachment to a landscape is registered analogously by his use of arbitrary colors—the way the hues of tree trunks abruptly shift from terra-cotta to blue, and the blocks of leaves are at once summer green, autumn yellow, and midnight blue (fig. 12). But there is a fine line: overindulged mannerisms and affectations can be called jazzy, a pejorative. A first-rate voice isn't required; Ella Fitzgerald had one, Billie Holiday did not. The emotional affect of a performance is central, and very arguable. The *Pennies from Heaven* promotional record proffers defining distinctions. On side B, Frances Langford, Armstrong, and Bing Crosby each sing one chorus of the title tune with Jimmy Dorsey's Orchestra. There are no exchanges between them, as though this were an audition tape.

Frances Langford sings the number so properly that nothing can distract us from the mediocrity of the lyrics and melody. "Every time it rains, it rains pennies from heaven / Don't you know each cloud contains pennies from heaven? / You'll find your fortune falling all over town / Be sure that your umbrella is upside down," sings Langford, too briskly, almost eliding the lines where only dramatic pauses if not rhythmic phrasing would let listeners absorb the message of a song that immediately became a Depression-era anthem of positive thinking, along with "When You're Smiling," "Life Is Just a Bowl of Cherries," and "Let's Face the Music and Dance." Crosby, already moving away from jazz, sings the lyrics too earnestly, even pompously, which makes his few liberties very conspicuous. When he sings the first two title phrases, "pennies from heaven," he drops his voice, a familiar Armstrong tack, but it's jazzy, coming too early in the number to make any dramatic point. Armstrong respects the melody completely, more than Crosby, and sings with a degree of conviction and fervor intelligently geared to the song's vernacular imagery, its "sunshine and flowers" (a subsequent trope). Armstrong's principal liberty is rhythmic compression: he lets three beats pass between each line—a definite caesura— where Crosby allows barely one beat. This phrasing isolates and vivifies the song's modest imagery, giving it some of the weight we deserve. Only jazz singing could do this for "Pennies from Heaven." Mel Tormé sang it Armstrong's way in his 1994 album, *A Tribute to Bing Crosby.*

Of the three vocalists, only Armstrong makes us consider and visualize the closing image of the trawling umbrella. An immense movie theater lobby poster of it—imagine numerous glinting medallion-size gold coins bouncing around in the upturned open umbrella—would cheer up any drab Depression room, as in Walker Evans's 1935 photograph of the bleak interior of a West Virginia coal miner's house. There, two large cardboard cutout store-display ads of a smiling young man and woman in graduation gowns and a Santa Claus hefting a frosty Coke are supposed to brighten the miserable wall, a virtual found collage. The broom is upside down—head up, that is, very proper, to look better for Evans's camera. "I want to live in a world where the songs come true," says Arthur (Steve Martin), a forlorn sheet-music salesman slumped over the lunch counter, fedora pulled low, frozen in a cinematic tableau vivant of Edward Hopper's *Nighthawks* (1942), one of several overt Evans and Hopper setups in *Pennies from Heaven* (1981), Dennis Potter's melancholy movie fantasia of thirties songs, each of which inspires a theatrical routine in step with music's place as a

61. Walker Evans, *Interior Detail, West Virginia Coal Miner's House,* 1935. This and subsequent Evans pictures here were photographed for the Farm Security Administration (FSA) and published in Evans' book *American Photographs* (1938).

BLUEBIRD

Electrically
PHONOGRAPH

Recorded
RECORDS

Not Licensed for   Radio Broadcast

WHITE HEAT–Fox Trot
(Will Hudson)
Jimmie Lunceford and his Orchestra
B-5713-A

©RCA Manufacturing Co., Inc., Camden, N.J.U.S.A.

RCA

62. 1934 record label.

Depression relief agency. A young audiophile of 2002, dwelling in his or her multimedia paradise, doesn't know that sixty-five years ago a recording artist's ten-inch, two-sided 78-rpm shellac discs were issued singly every two or so months, and once purchased, never idly—there was a Depression—they became the center of a kind of attention and concentration without equal today. Even the graphic designs of record labels were symbolically optimistic, Bluebird projecting Brancusi's *Bird{s} in Space* flight plan (fig. 62) while OKeh repeated the "red weather" of Wallace Stevens, Derain, and Matisse (fig. 13).

Armstrong sings the songs as though they could materialize. His seemingly unrefined voice only makes him more credible, sincerity being concomitant with imperfection and awkwardness, or so many people believe, to pinpoint the appeal of folk art ("outsider art" is its current tag). The critics who have lamented the limited range and quality of Armstrong's voice have missed or misunderstood a crucial aspect of his art and craftiness. In the thirties (the first decade of his great success), Armstrong would occasionally record a slow number in a clear, lovely tenor voice (e.g., Ellington's "Solitude," 1935; the spiritual "Nobody Knows the Trouble I've Seen," 1938), artistic "lapses" on his part that prove that his gravelly voice was a deliberate strategy, an exaggerated Expressionist "impurity" calculated to balance or compensate for his nonpareil brilliance as a trumpeter. (Eventually his voice did coarsen.) Great technique alone would only elevate and distance him. But Armstrong's choice of the gravelly voice cast him as Everyman. "I can sing as good as that," thinks an average Joe, accepting and responding to Armstrong as his manly agent in matters of the heart, expressed openly, without embarrassment. (Doesn't this happen with other affecting male singers of limited technique, all instrumentalists, including Jack Teagarden, Hoagy Carmichael, Bunny Berigan, Joe Mooney, Oran "Hot Lips" Page, Jimmy Rowles, and Dave Frishberg? Woody Herman? Almost, but he's a bit too good. Chet Baker is too effete.) Armstrong the singer is at once a self-conscious primitivist and great actor. He hit the nail on the head when he described himself as "actor" on a 1932 passport application, after having appeared in only the first of his twenty-four films (1931–69). "He turns 'yeast' into 'yeats,'" Cole Porter might have written, to be sung by Bobby Short. Is he a jazz singer? No, because he respects the songs too much—the tradition of *Lieder*.

Armstrong's dramatic sincerity as a vocalist overrides the varying offensiveness of his consistently dubious or deplorable racial/racist material. Witness his winsome, lyrical treatment of the archetypal plantation number "When It's Sleepy Time Down South" (1931), which became his theme song. Its highly colored stock images ("banjos ringing," "mammies singing," "steamboats splashing," "soft winds blowing through the pinewood trees") cumulatively emit a rich, primary glow, as in a folk painting, in part because the song's composers, Leon and Otis René, were a knowing Creole brother team from New Orleans who managed to mine the down-home mother lode in Hollywood during the thirties and forties. When Armstrong sings, "You needn't tell me because I *know* when it's sleepy time down South," his open-voweled, upturned delivery of the verb *no-o-uh* convinces us that he does, quite happily. His soulful rhetorical turns convincingly beget vernacular images of harmony and felicity that, however racist and false they now appear, conceivably brought comfort to Negroes who had participated in the Great Migration but had not found a Promised Land in the industrialized North. "When It's Sleepy Time Down South" and the more racially compromised "Carry Me Back to Old Virginny" (recorded in 1937 by Armstrong and the Mills Brothers) are, on one level, Norman Rockwell for Negroes afflicted by disappointment and urban anxieties. The muted, melancholy colors of Jacob Lawrence's superb *The Migration of the Negro* — 1940–41, a cycle of sixty images— seem to project the migrants' future as well as past travails.

"That's My Home" (1932), also composed by the René brothers, and premiered by Armstrong, wants to remind hope-filled, horizontally mobile Negroes that the Southern abodes they left behind, however humble, remain a sanctuary forever—drawing on the fact that elderly Negroes often did return there after many disappointing years in the urban North. "Carry Me Back"—alas, alack. Armstrong the vocalist goes home by dropping an octave as he sings the word "shack," thereby adding a basement bunker—a safe place in case of a big storm or a Klan raid, central heating by homemaker Armstrong. The homebound Mills Brothers faithfully sing, "There's where I labored so hard for dear ol' massa / Day after day in the fields of yeller corn / No place on earth do I love more sincerely / Than old Virginny, the state where I was born." Armstrong musters some dignity by changing "this old darkie's heart" to "the" and "dear ol' massa" to a carefully enunciated "old master." Walker Evans' 1936 detail of a minstrel showbill allows that dignity was not unsalvageable, though he achieves this only by improvising like a jazzman, tightly cropping the original "number," which included a very theatrical menacing villain just to the left and cacophonous large-lettered information about the show (fig. 63).

Armstrong even overrides the lowest verbal/visual caricature of a coon song. "Snowball, don't you melt away / 'Cause your daddy loves those dark brown eyes," Armstrong sings of the black baby named "Snowball" in the song of that title (1933). The warmth of Armstrong's paternal delivery dissipates the condescension of the racist name-humor then endemic in the popular arts: Farina, the pickaninny in the *Our Gang* movie shorts, or Whitewash Jones, the name of a black draftee in Abbott and Costello's *Buck Privates* (1941). Negro stage names in Hollywood such as Stepin Fetchit and Mantan Moreland (Charlie Chan's chauffeur) are of course wretched, yet the actors' eyeball-popping "comic" routines circa 1940 as cowards paralyzed by noises in the dark ("Feets, don't fail me now!")—racist enough, it seems—had earlier proved hilarious to all-black vaudeville audiences in the North who saw them as a right-on burlesque of the heebie-jeebies, those unsophisticated down-home folk fears of hauntings, ghosts, and voodoo curses. Racial material can turn out to be as multifaceted and perplexing as a Cubist painting. "Carry Me Back to Old Virginny," vintage minstrel stuff (1878), sold very well to blacks—not, one guesses, because of Armstrong's modest modern adjustments.

As calculated products of mass culture, Armstrong's plantation numbers should be seen in the widest context of popular, pastoral Depression-era art, especially Rockwell, other *Saturday Evening Post* illustrators, the homey comic strip *Gasoline Alley* (by Frank King), and the representational and willfully rustic painters of the American Scene/regionalist school such as Grant Wood, Thomas Hart Benton, and John Steuart Curry. *LIFE* magazine, which ignored modern art, often reproduced their work, and that of amateur small-town painters who were thought by academics and city-slicker editors alike to capture folk values convincingly. Walker Evans, who taught most everyone how to look at the American quotidian, found and photographed much better "naive" art—works that touchingly and amusingly document the basic human impulse to create art, to decorate and enhance one's environment. "When art can hold its own with prize cows, it is in a healthy state," declares the opening sentence of the sidebar text in a *LIFE* picture-spread titled "RURAL ART" (the capitalized letters are composed of little logs), sub-headed "Flowering of Art by Wisconsin Farmers Beheld at University's 'Farm and Home' Week" (March 31, 1941, the year the Depression ended fiscally). *LIFE*'s Wisconsin images of moonlight and rivers generically complement "When It's Sleepy Time Down South" and Waller's "Old Plantation." The magazine's pro-

63. Walker Evans, *Minstrel Showbill Detail*, Alabama, 1936.

grammatic and fulsome pastoralism, already drafted to support the coming war, resembles the official state-sponsored folkish art of the Soviets and Nazi Germany; at its best, the pastoralism looks back to such nineteenth-century artists as Frederick Edwin Church and ahead to Hoagy Carmichael's buttermilk skies. How often will the modernist in Armstrong be able to cut through the goo? Scramble or bake it? (Romy Golan's 1995 *Modernity and Nostalgia: Art and Politics in France Between the Wars* is an excellent study of the retrograde, reactionary appeal of bucolic realism.) *LIFE*'s 1941 color reproduction of a mediocre painting of a stolid, heavy-limbed brown horse looming over a dim landscape is captioned, " 'Oil' is Emelia Snyder's title for this lordly Belgian stallion standing firm as a church on Wisconsin soil." Consecrated ground is ready for war. "She seemed to think that it must steady him to look at a buffalo" (in a zoo), Nathanael West writes of the treacly Betty in *Miss Lonelyhearts* (1933), in the chapter "Miss Lonely-hearts in the Country," a timeless lampoon of the curative powers of American pastoral, from Stephen Foster to Ansel Adams and Marlboro Country.

Armstrong's 1967 recording of "What a Wonderful World" is also historically apt, a putative antidote to the depressing sight of campus and urban disorder over war and race. Armstrong devotees who lament the probability that most younger listeners know him only as the singer of this trumpet-free number, resurrected by the film *Good Morning, Vietnam* (1987), fail to perceive that "What a Wonderful World" is consistent with the earlier pastoralism that is at the core of Armstrong and his populist appeal. The song should also be valued for the way it revived interest in him. "I see skies of blue, and clouds of white, / The bright blessed day, the dark sacred night," he sings, with enough conviction to lower the calorie-count of the lyrics. They're not Robert Frost, but people without recourse to poetry also have miles to go. "It's sleepy time" as an isolated phrase is childspeak, and Armstrong would simply will felicity and a good night's sleep.

Evans and Armstrong, very different kinds of men, provide numerous benchmark examples of dignity conferred on humble man-made structures and musical fakelore, such as the pseudo-spiritual "Lawd, You Made the Night Too Long" (1932), words and music by two white Tin Pan Alley veterans, Sam M. Lewis and Victor Young. Armstrong opens "Lawd" by declaiming three loud, churchly "Hallelujahs" that are serious and floorboard-rattling. "You made the river flow / The flowers grow," he sings, his throbbing sincerity turning virtual dog-

64. Poster for *Hallelujah,* movie musical about Negro life on a Southern plantation, directed by King Vidor, 1929.

65. Walker Evans, *Negro Church, South Carolina,* 1936. Bing Crosby and Guy Lombardo each recorded "Lawd, You Made the Night Too Long" at the same time as Armstrong. Simple faith has appeal to modernists, too, if the expressive form is austere enough and has a human face.

66. Pablo Picasso, *Man,* 1958. Wood. Almost 4′ high. Does literal transparency equal good character? Or has he lost his head to sex? The title, also bald, makes this a witty mock-humanist statement about phallocentric man. He's a work of art, to judge by the frame, the equivalent of the Armstrong grin that's supposed to excuse anything.

gerel into vernacular poetry. "I got a heart / I got a cabin / The door is wide open," Armstrong continues, his impassioned delivery making us accept the cabin metaphor as the truth about his open, loving nature. He was mainly known as "Pops," not "Satchmo," to musicians everywhere. Photographer Evans, however, was a reserved and sardonic frustrated writer (to whom Flaubert was God) from a genteel Midwestern family who'd had scant social contact with black people. His 1935–36 FSA photos of the deep South include only a few blacks, observed at a distance. Yet his quietly empathetic 1936 picture of a Negro church in South Carolina captures a rich sense of the congregation's collective faith (fig. 65). Evans succeeded by choosing to photograph the church from a perfect frontal angle at a perfect time of day, when the numinous light on the eloquently plain belfry was just so and the shadow across the front accentuated its resemblance to a foursquare face, a veritable Picasso assemblage (fig. 66) with windows wide-eyed before the Lord and a door that silently mouths "Hallelujah!"

Armstrong's compassion for unlikely people as well as poor songs is tested by "Just a Gigolo" (1931), where he is called upon to sing the dirge of a gigolo who confronts mortality. "Oh, I'm just a gigolo," he sings, offering a job description of a figure more familiar to audiences then as a touchstone of decadence and soulless male opportunism. "Paid for every dance / Selling each romance / Every night some heart betraying," sings Armstrong. But the lyrics actually don't sound as lugubrious or maudlin as they look on the page, because Armstrong expresses his natural affinity and sympathy for night people, predicated on the harsh circumstances of his youth: born out of wedlock to a fifteen-year-old girl; abandoned immediately by his father; raised in the roughest, most squalid section of New Orleans; committed to the Colored Waifs Home at age fifteen; married, for the first time at seventeen, to a teenaged prostitute.

Armstrong expresses his compassionate open (cabin) door policy in "Just a Gigolo" with a poignant muted trumpet solo that, backed by a mandolin, respects the melody completely, every note of it, and breaks your heart. Dare one say that anymore? (Miles Davis's muted "Bye-Bye Blackbird" solo of 1956 has the same effect. A son of Pops, after all, despite his affectless stage persona.) "There will come a day," sings Armstrong, "Youth will pass away . . . [and] when the end comes, I know," Armstrong concludes, "They'll say 'Just another *jig* I know' / As life goes on without me." Although the ad-libbed racial pun ("jig" for "jigaboo," synonymous with "nigger") may not rank with Joycean wordplay, its depth of feeling takes no back seat to any expressive efforts, "high" or "low." If Armstrong's vocal makes the doleful lyrics worthy of an open coffin, his trumpet solo is an Irish wake. He doubles the tempo crisply, an invitation to eat, drink, and dance—a jig, of course.

Recorded at the same session as "Just a Gigolo," Armstrong's "Shine" *is* Joycean. Before any close discussion of it, however, "Shine" must be placed in the context of Armstrong's recordings of the early thirties. By 1931 he was a megastar, as we say now, performing and recording arrangements that featured him as a singer and a virtuosic soloist backed by big bands, a departure from the small-group performances of 1925–28 that established his reputation and are usually (and wrongly) said to be the peak of his art. (Armstrong's Hot Five and Hot Seven were recording, not performing, units, and during this period he made his living as featured player in big bands led by other men.) Armstrong now turned from his black jazz/blues repertoire to pop songs, a shift consistent with an important professional promotion, in both senses of the word, as OKeh Records moved Armstrong from its "race" to its mainstream (white) label in late 1929. (OKeh's black "race" series bore numbers in an 8000 sequence, while the "white" records were in the 40000 sequence. The original numbers appear in the liner or booklet notes of every LP and CD and are of no small historic interest.) Armstrong thrived in the mainstream. His masterful recordings of "Caucasian" compositions that were not yet standards (some had just been written) bespeak the excellent taste and intelligence of a self-aware, serious musician rather than the intuitions of a folk genius.

The songs from 1930–31 alone include Gershwin's "I Got Rhythm," Harold Arlen's "Between the Devil and the Deep Blue Sea," Johnny Green's "Body and Soul," Jimmy McHugh's "Exactly Like You" and "On the Sunny Side of the Street," and Hoagy Carmichael's "Star Dust," "Rockin' Chair," and "Georgia On My Mind." All of these grand songs are by white men—not a minor point, given the segregated circumstances of jazz as well as society at large. When Armstrong quotes from Gershwin's *Rhapsody in Blue* (1924), a work that was only five years old, in his trumpet solo on the Waller-Razaf song "Ain't Misbehavin' " (Armstrong's nightly show-stopper in *Hot Chocolates*), the transparent allusion at once posits racial integration and a generous impulse quite foreign to current racial politics, where it is *de rigueur* to wax bitter about *Rhapsody in Blue* as a vile act of cultural misappropriation by Gershwin and his premier conductor, the well-named (Paul) Whiteman—crime and pun. And if you're smiling, and your grim life seems brighter now, if only for a moment, then we've successfully telescoped the mission of Armstrong, Waller, and Ellington, whose clarinetist, Barney Bigard (a charter member of Armstrong's All Stars), quotes *Rhapsody in Blue* during his solo on Duke's "The Saddest Tale" (1934). Armstrong's quotation of Gershwin on one of his last "race" records surely limns his ambition to build bridges through music—a worn metaphor to suit the unpretentiousness of the man, who was anything but naive when it came to the business of communication.

To compensate for the more formal, mainstream, and "multicultural" aspects of his new music, the Armstrong of 1930–33 engaged in a calculated and unique effort to narrow the psychic distance between himself and his home listeners, who now included white people as never before, as well as black folks who had to be kept in the fold. Phonograph records and radios represented the only way most blacks were going to enter white homes. "Now, ladies and gentlemen, we have a little novelty for you this evening," Armstrong says to his invisible audience at the outset of two records ("Chinatown, My Chinatown" in 1931 and "New Tiger Rag" in 1932). He tries to keep blacks in the fold by occasionally employing their secret vocabulary. "Get a load of this viper's language," he says in "Sweet Sue, Just You" (1933), as he and Budd Johnson are about to sing some charming nonsense. A "viper" was a marijuana smoker—Armstrong was an avid lifelong inhaler— and the delirious singing seems to document their "high." Armstrong and his black listeners knew that few whites would understand this jive, the joke's on them, dig it, can you keep a secret?

Now we're side by side with Armstrong, walking on some Northern city street at the outset of his first recording of "When It's Sleepy Time Down South." "There's a guy comin' up the street look like he's from my home town," he tells us, conversationally. "Look like ol' Charlie Alexander, man. Why I believe it is! What you say, Gate?" Charlie: "What you say, Dipper?" Armstrong: "How long you been up here, boy?" "Oh, I been up here about a year and a half." Armstrong: ". . . Man, I been up here a long time myself . . . I'm going back home . . . I'm going, gettin' some of them red beans and [do you] . . . remember them sweet potatoes?" Elevated by a subtle African-American union—the beat of their speech and the Hemingwayesque repetition of "been up here"— Armstrong's nostalgia personalizes and vivifies the threadbare vernacular lyrics and drives the song home. The spoken introduction is omitted from Armstrong's many subsequent recordings of the number. "Now we're gonna take you all the way down to New Orleans, my home town . . . for one of those street parades," he announces at the start of "High Society" (1933), solid information for new white listeners unfamiliar with this New Orleans jazz warhorse. "Look out!" Armstrong warns. His marching band is ready to roll and can't be expected to make sudden stops if a small child darts in front of them.

Armstrong asks the listeners at home to build on their visual and visceral sense of him, grinning or grimacing, and to eavesdrop on the bandstand as he talks comprehensible jive to the cats in the band: "So get your chops together, boys, while we mug lightly, slightly, and politely," he says in "Chinatown, My Chinatown." (Waller's verbal interjections don't draw us in this way; it's enough if we join the fun, wherever we're seated.) Armstrong verbally kicks off the tempo—"one, two!"—on several numbers, including two superb Harold Arlen songs, "I've Got the World on a String" (1933) and "I Gotta Right to Sing the Blues" (1933). "Look like they're after me!" he says with mock fearfulness of the riffing, surging saxophone section. He introduces us to the members of the band by name, sometimes saying what town they're from. He offers precise musical instructions—"Bring it out, bring it out, sax-oh-*phones!*" He encourages the band—"Charlie Alexander, swing out on them ivories, boy!"—and comments on their playing— "Beautiful!" "Oh!" "Uh, *huh!*" "Way down, way down!"—and he is in turn exhorted by one of them: "Take off, Gate!" You are there. Armstrong is the most *phonogenic* recording artist. He invented self-reflexive phonography, with an assist from Jelly Roll Morton, the first to gab on a disc about his own band.

"Boy, am I riffin' this evenin'," Armstrong says in the midst of a solo, and the old-fashioned single microphone setup probably would not have picked this up for a "live" audience. "What's the matter with you, boy?" he says, about to sing Harold Arlen. "Don't you know I gotta right to sing the blues?" We are privileged to hear these asides because we seem to have some kind of miraculous access to Armstrong's space; and the procedure is analogous to the ways in which Joyce and Faulkner and avant-garde photographers of the day employ intimate or inexplicable vantage points (Feininger's view of the Bauhaus jazz band, fig. 67) to imply or take us into extraordinary corners of consciousness. "Ain't that right, little trumpet? Say *'yes sir!'* Oh, that little devil," Armstrong chuckles in "Chinatown, My Chinatown," trying to bring his horn to life for us. "The piano has to jazz," exclaims Fats Waller, announcing a solo, and pretending that *his* instrument has a life of its own. Armstrong wants his alive music to enter our living room, in the deepest sense. Logic dictates that Feininger's musicians have been observed from the perspective of one of the fat, floating notes just emitted by the trombone.

"Laughin' Louie," from 1933, is a kind of entr'acte recording that pauses to take mordant account of the artifice of Armstrong's phonography. Armstrong enthusiasts and scholars alike have long been baffled by this number—put off, no doubt, by the master's self-mockery, which they won't even acknowledge. The orchestra opens the number uptempo, and before Armstrong can do anything, the band intones, as a choir, "Yes! You're the fastest, Louie," and everyone laughs, including the leader. "Now, ladies and gentlemen . . . I gotta do some practicin' on this Selmer trumpet," Armstrong announces, compromising his genial informality by mentioning the brand name as though he were appearing on a sponsored radio show. He sings the phrase "I'm Laughin' Louie" five times, pronouncing it the way the public always did, as opposed to Armstrong himself, who pronounced his name as "Lew-is." The ambitious, calculating, market-driven "Louie" is his own target. He plugs Selmer, the manufacturer of his trumpet, one more time, and sings, "The reason why I laugh" every morning is that "I see my photograph" on the wall. So much for natural joy and humor.

The band's mirth grows decidedly, as in the old comic routine of contagious, anarchic laughter. (Laurel and Hardy, who often employed the routine, do their best one in *Fra Diavolo,* also a 1933 release.) "Take off, Gate!" shouts one of Armstrong's musicians, an exhortation that sounds more spontaneous on several previous Armstrong records, as the band's laughter suggests. He plays one note only. "Mel-low!" yells another musician sarcastically, and everyone laughs at the hollow compliment, including the trumpet virtuoso himself. He pauses dramatically—what next?—and then plays the same single note again, a comical anticlimax. "Watch out there, Pops!" exults another bandsman. Everyone laughs hard, since the enthusiasm is, of course, unwarranted and facetious, exactly pitched to the entire number's droll send-up of contrived ebullience. Armstrong is as self-conscious as the Saul Steinberg artist who is practicing his mandalas with joyless, comic doggedness (fig. 68). Parody or self-parody, as Proust says, is a cleansing exercise. Then Armstrong plays part of an opera-like number, unaccompanied and rubato, as though he were in his dressing room, warming up for a performance. It's a technically demanding, non-jazz

67. Lux Feininger, *Untitled* (Bauhaus jazz band), c. 1929.

fragment, which he executes flawlessly. He ends it on a dangerously high note, as primed and tense as Joe Louis about to go out and fight for the title.

"Shine," which draws strength from the convincing, collective intimacy of all the Armstrong you've heard, becomes even more powerful if you "read" it as act two, so to speak, in a dramatic, two-sided rejection of "Just another jig I know," akin to Armstrong's 1929 rescue of the uncharacteristic Waller-Razaf "(What Did I Do to Be So) Black and Blue," the B-side of "Ain't Misbehavin'." Armstrong turned "Black and Blue" into a stirring "protest" song by dropping the verse as first sung and recorded by Edith Wilson in *Hot Chocolates,* in which she moans that her dark complexion costs her lovers: "Brown and yellows / All have fellows / Gentlemen prefer them light," a significant echo of Anita Loos's famous 1925 title. Armstrong's "editing" buried this verse forever in order to highlight the protest—subversive editing, considering that the record, on OKeh's "race" label, was aimed at blacks. The message is deemed so important that for once Armstrong skips his trumpet improvisation. It's his version of "Black and Blue" that the narrator of Ralph Ellison's *Invisible Man* (1952) carries with him when he goes underground.

Armstrong's regressive and deathly use of "jig" in the penultimate line of "Just a Gigolo" (it is offered as an epitaph) verbally concludes the first side of the original 78-rpm record, backed by "Shine," whose egregious lyrics seem to be a logical and awful extension of the self-abnegation of the one pejorative word "jig." (The two songs have been paired successively this way in systematic Armstrong reissues over the years, including *Louis Armstrong, Volume 7: You're Driving Me Crazy,* on Columbia, which also includes several of the other numbers mentioned here.) The vocal on "Shine" is never discussed by critics, but it deserves a close listen and analysis.

"Shine" is generically a coon song, its music and lyrics by Ford Dabney and Cecil Mack (aka Richard McPherson), well-educated Negroes with excellent musical credentials, not least Dabney's membership in the elite Clef Club. Armstrong's vocal on "Shine" evolves in three stages. First, the lyrics are sung complete, Armstrong as the shine: "'Cause my hair is curly / Just because my teeth are pearly / Just because I always wear a smile," sings Armstrong. "Smile," obviously, is the signal word, but the perfect grammar is a surprising element that seems to save the performer from total caricature, now more than ever, given our sociopolitical sensitivities. Respected Negro poets of the

68. Saul Steinberg, untitled drawing from his book of drawings and graphic caprices, *The New World*, 1965.

time, such as Paul Laurence Dunbar and Langston Hughes, both of whom used dialect freely, would have revised the lyric: "Just because my teeth is pearly" is accurate, and "wear" needs an "s." ("I bought a new hat, sho' is fine, but I wish I had back that old gal o' mine." Amos 'n' Andy 'n' pals? No, Langston Hughes, four elided lines from his poem "Dressed Up" [1926], the year that *Amos 'n' Andy,* created and performed by two white men, premiered on the radio.) The well-spoken shine of Dabney and Mack's song is, on second thought, very strange, a kind of schizophrenic construct and amalgam that projects another angle of W. E. B. Du Bois's famous theory of Negro "double consciousness," the paradoxical literate/illiterate "bilingual" mentalities that he discussed in *The Souls of Black Folk* (1903). "I ain't rough!" Armstrong had insisted in a 1928 "race" record Armstrong titled "I'm Not Rough," whose correct title grammar documents Du Bois's idea with sly wit.

"I take troubles with a smile," Armstrong continues in "Shine." His (or the shine's) grammar is still as firm as a Tuskegee man's. "Just because my color is shady / Mmm, different maybe / That's why they call me—" But instead of intoning the racist title epithet "shine," Armstrong substitutes scat jabberwocky (though not in the film version of the number). He traduces the song with a nonsense lingo that turns out to make perfect ethical sense.

In the second stage of the song, the only intelligible phrases include "hair is curly" and "teeth are pearly." Armstrong's scat attack bounces the phrases around like grotesquely sprung eyeballs in some of Picasso's preliminary drawings for *Guernica* (1937); flying body parts and vectors in comic-strip brawls and Tex Avery's animated cartoons of the forties; and *The Nightmare of the White Elephant* in Matisse's *Jazz* (fig. 69). The third intelligible isolated phrase, "Just because," introduces "Shine" 's third and most radical vocal phase: pure scat. And this rejects the possibility that there are any just or justifiable "becauses" in regard to the racial stereotyping of the song or the culture that fosters it, black songwriters included.

Thus, the lyrics of "Shine" have been deconstructed and destroyed. The scat interlude concludes with the complete line "That's why they call me *shine,*" the offensive word restored and emphasized as the target, really, of Armstrong's concluding trumpet solo, sonic assault that features a perfectly played half-valve glissando during which the tempo halts momentarily, and Armstrong is suddenly like a great heavyweight boxer—Joe Louis against Max Schmeling—who has cornered his opponent and is now setting him up for the knockout crescendo, a brilliant ascending run whose fast, high, full-bodied clarion blows do the trick. "Mercy! Stop that fight!" Fats Waller would have shouted if he had been at the piano accompanying his friend on this recording. At least one coon song has bit the dust. The jig is up. "Bump! Bump! Bump! That's the curse right back at you!" exclaims Waller at the end of "The Curse of an Aching Heart" (1936). "*Sssst! Plooey!* . . . insides and brains all scattered round," Powerhouse says of Gypsy. The Negro lower class, represented here by Armstrong, has leveled the dicty (black idiom for "snobbish," "very proper," "hypocritical") Negro middle class, represented here by the composers of "Shine," or what's left of it. The big, flat cartoon teeth of Covarrubias's Armstrong are equal to the dehumanizing lyrics of this darky number while Armstrong's demonic cartoon frown and furious eyes register the rage behind the mask worn by the modern minstrels known as Satchmo and Powerhouse. Only "My Window Faces the South" hints at such rage in Waller, though his funereal recordings on pipe organ of the spirituals "Deep River" and "Sometimes I Feel Like a Motherless Child" plumb a sensibility capacious enough for anything.

Armstrong's scat attack on "Shine" represents a sharp irony inasmuch as "primitive" (nonverbal or preverbal) vocalizing has been able to dispatch "civilized" (verbal) discourse. Armstrong the singer moves in the same direction in his 1931 recording of the most popular American ballad, Hoagy Carmichael's "Star Dust." It was being called "immortal" as early as 1939. Composed as a brisk piano rag inspired by Bix Beiderbecke's cornet style, "Star Dust" didn't receive lyrics for two years, and Armstrong's vocal underscores the vacuity of Mitchell Parish's very purple words. Very appropriately, he also wrote the lyrics for "Deep Purple." An astral specialist, Parish followed with "Stars Fell on Alabama" and "Stairway to the Stars," a title that projects any singer's uphill struggle with triteness. (Carmichael recorded "Star Dust" six times over the years, but sang the lyrics only once.) "You're in my arms," declares the song, "The nightingale told its fairy tale / Of paradise where roses grew," which is either a "poetic" evocation of orgasm or nothing. Armstrong states in effect that it's nothing. He

OVERLEAF: 69. Henri Matisse, *The Nightmare of the White Elephant,* from *Jazz,* 1947.

drops his voice when delivering "roses grew," as if to say that these flowers are dead. The song's famous opening line, "Sometimes I wonder why I spend each lonely night," is acceptable enough, but Armstrong daringly sings every word on the same note, no doubt to emphasize the loneliness—the figurative single note—which he answers and symbolically eases with visceral vocal sounds.

Armstrong's earthy "Star Dust" eroticizes Parish's euphemistic, chaste lyrics with an amusing and stirring series of grunts, groans, muffled words, elided phrases, and a discernible "mama" and "oh, *baby.*" (Lee Morgan brilliantly transferred this tumbling vocal gaiety to his bebop trumpet in the 1960s, a rare feat, especially in jazz's most angry and bitter decade.) "*Ooo, ooo, ooo,* what a little moonlight can do-oo," sings Armstrong's best student, Billie Holiday, age twenty, vivifying the trashy "What a Little Moonlight Can Do" (1935), formulating, too, the continuum, the cultural *and* musical legacy of Armstrong, the founding father and fount of inspiration wherever one turns—the greatest melodist and the best accompanist of blues singers, as in his recordings with Bessie Smith in the twenties.

Although Armstrong appears as accompanist on more than one hundred recordings by female blues singers, and made several charming single discs and albums with Ella Fitzgerald, he never sustained a memorable collaboration with a first-rate female singer. For this we turn to Billie Holiday and Lester Young, the Eve and Adam of modern jazz singing and tenor saxophone playing. Each bestowed upon the other their famous nicknames: "the President" or "Prez" (of the saxophone) and "Lady Day," a two-word poem to describe her dignified, almost motionless posture as a singer and the way her delivery at once expressed and pierced fogbanks of melancholy and nightclub smoke.

Their sense of time, as subtle and flexible as any instrumentalist's has ever been, always involves playing off the basic beat—the monotonous clump-clump-clump of the foursquare 1930s—floating ahead of it, falling behind, then catching up and pulling ahead again, despite the dead weight of most bass lines then. This tonic tug-of-war builds upon the driving but flexible rhythms of Armstrong, or the Landlord, as Billie always called Armstrong—"You know," she once explained, "he owns the building." To describe the rhythms of Young and Holiday properly is to find an art book that accurately reproduces Mondrian's wide range of "whites" (the word is unsatisfactory) or grays—the Whistler-like tonal scale of the Holiday-Young palette where Armstrong favored the equivalent of red, orange, yellow, and every hue of blue. When Young and Holiday solo back to back, without interruption, as on "I Must Have That Man" and "This Year's Kisses" (from their first recording session, 1937), the eerie closeness of their light and airy tones is emphasized, pointing to the idea of the soulmate, and the fact that Lester actually roomed with Billie and her mother for a time, though he and Billie were never lovers—a striking, exceptional fact given the free and easy jazz milieu.

The two performed together steadily for several months in 1937, when Holiday sang with Count Basie's band, a wonderful warm-up for the forty small-band recordings they made together, 1937–41, under her name or Teddy Wilson's, with sublime groups composed of the best jazz musicians of the 1930s, drawn mainly from the big bands of Basie, Ellington, Goodman, and Cab Calloway. Young takes great solos on many of these records, including "The Man I Love," "Foolin' Myself," and "Mean to Me"—the titles arranged in this progression to put Holiday's amorous life in a nutshell. Their most moving and musically amazing collaborations, such as "I'll Never Be the Same" (1937), redefine the conception of "accompanist." Instead of playing trenchant little fill-ins behind Billie, like Armstrong or Joe Smith backing Bessie Smith, Lester solos nonstop, modestly off-mike, creating soft countermelodies that weave in and around her melodic lines, sometimes running parallel or merging with them for a measure or two, telepathically anticipating the harmonic liberties and shifts in pitch that Billie—a jazz improviser of genius—is going to take with the tune in question.

The tunes are often questionable indeed, Tin Pan Alley trifles such as "Born to Love," "Without Your Love," "Who Wants Love?", and "Me, Myself, and I" (all 1937), whose transformation by Holiday-Young once again evokes the modernist enterprise of collage and assemblage, making her queen of the ragpickers. (She made some one hundred other small-group records without Young in the 1930s, everything collected in the monumental ten-CD Columbia Legacy collection of 2001, *Lady Day.*) "Me, myself, and I / We're all in love with you," she sings, and the joyfulness of her declamation turns the trite, greeting-card pronoun cluster into a convincing expression of love carried to the nth power, the three pronouns sounding like sprinters in a track meet. (This Billie Holiday is a total surprise to listeners who know only her wan work of the 1950s, when she had become our Edith Piaf.) "It can't be denied / You brought the sun to us," she continues, lifted further by Lester's nonstop descant and Buck Clayton's warm, Armstrong-

70. Prez, photograph by Otto Hess, 1938.

influenced trumpet solo. They bring on the sun and the moon, too, in the next song they recorded that day, "A Sailboat in the Moonlight," a big hit for Guy Lombardo, who led the corniest dance band as far as jazz fans were concerned, though Armstrong was not alone among black jazz musicians in his admiration for Lombardo's unjazzy band, its respect for melody and its ability to set just the right tempo—dancing was a community activity then, bringing up to ten thousand people together on the dance floor, as at the Hollywood Palladium.

The most ebullient of the Holiday-Young rescue operations, "A Sailboat in the Moonlight" is possibly more memorable for the extreme vacuity of its lyrics by Guy's brother Carmen Lombardo (of "Sweethearts on Parade"), music by John Jacob Loeb. Stiffly sung by Carmen himself on the Lombardos' record, the lyrics represent a challenge to Lester to shine even brighter in order to keep the word-burdened boat afloat. "A Sailboat in the Moonlight" imagines a dreamy "heaven just for two" coming true on a balmy night beneath a June moon. Waller would have looked skyward as he dispatched all this to dead-song heaven. But Holiday sings "A Sailboat to Moonlight" with her customary perfect articulation, and an affecting sincerity, like Armstrong's, which projects *her* genuine sense of yearning, however childish the lyrics and rhyme. "The things that I long for are few," she sings, certainly an acceptable, even poignant line—a corny, old-fashioned Hallmark card ringing true, conferring ballast to "A Sailboat in the Moonlight," as does the acrid pitch of Billie's voice, which almost always reduces or hardens the sap in her songs. Matisse's *Heart* also elevates a greeting-card cliché against all odds (fig. 72).

While Holiday is singing the banal lyrics, Lester Young's saxophone descant offers a simultaneous translation into a musical poetry equivalent to gentle caresses, warm winds, and the full sails that will carry them smoothly away. Imagine that Armstrong, thanks to current overdubbing electronic technology, is scatting behind one of his own vocals—an Armstrong who is literally her Pops, a completely loving rather than carnal presence, in keeping with proper paternity and the platonic love story of Prez and Lady Day. "The way Lester played behind her," says the pianist Jimmy Rowles, who knew them both very well, "she would feel like she was just in her mother's arms." As Billie sings the out-chorus of "A Sailboat in the Moonlight," heatedly, pushing the beat, Armstrong-like—she's the lead horn, too—it's every man for himself (Billie's well-named), no unison riff, the trumpet, clarinet, and tenor sax each taking off, more or less in the same direction, sail-

boats jibbing dangerously at dawn as the moon disappears in the Day light.

Holiday's hottest, most Armstrong-driven rhythm number is Gershwin's "Summertime," which only needs to be rescued from respectability (1936, Lester Young is not present). Her intense, medium-tempo recording is one of the earliest from *Porgy and Bess* (1935), which had just failed on Broadway. Her version still stands in its heat, alone, as a great but not crude vocal celebration of carnal vitality; only Sidney Bechet's keening 1939 recording on soprano saxophone rivals Holiday's "Summertime," though his is clouded midway by an interpolation of Verdi's *Miserere*. "Oh—your daddy's rich and your ma is good-lookin'," sings the folk-opera Bess, but only Lady Day's passionate recording makes you believe that they could conceive a child. Armstrong's rhythmic style serves the statuesque young woman perfectly where a lesser artist might stoop to vulgar affectations.

Holiday's conversion of Armstrong's relentless, syncopated beat turns into a kind of march tempo her second time through the lyrics so that "You—going to—rise up—singing" (to approximate her march through dry grass and bramble) threatens to ignite a brushfire, distant indeed from every subsequent snail's-pace "Summertime" vocal by a refined, operatic mezzo-soprano. Armstrong appears on Holiday's "Summertime," once removed, in the person of Bunny Berigan, the greatest Armstrong-influenced white trumpeter, who opens the record over rolling tom-toms with a deep-down, growly call to arms.

Colored gals could sing as they wished, since they were only a threat to the competition, other women. But Armstrong's entirely straightforward versions of love ballads such as "If I Could Be with You" (1930) are rarely eroticized for his expanded white audience. Armstrong's most intense and moving romantic singing of 1930–31 concerns melancholy ("Memories of You," "When Your Lover Has Gone"), submissiveness ("I Surrender, Dear"), rejection ("Blue Again"), and tragic loss ("Body and Soul") rather than courtship or pursuit, which saves his skin, as it were, as a commercial property, since the wrong kind of female-directed gaze from a colored man could end in a lynching. The title number of *Down Argentine Way* (1940) was one of

OPPOSITE: 71. Lady Day, photograph by William P. Gottlieb, n.d.

OVERLEAF: 72. Henri Matisse, *The Heart*, from *Jazz*, 1947.

the Nicholas Brothers' greatest performances, but they never appear in a scene with the film's blond star, Betty Grable. Only once do they dance with a woman—Dorothy Dandridge, a person of color, in *Sun Valley Serenade* (1941). Many insecure young white men preferred Bing Crosby to Frank Sinatra in the forties because the lethargic, middle-aged Crosby didn't represent any competition, any implied sexual threat to your date or sweetheart, and his role as a priest in two popular movies unmanned him further. Armstrong's slurring and blurring of the words to the provocative "All of Me" in 1931 protectively neutralize (or neuter) him as an imaginable sexual rival without altogether extinguishing the spirit of Eros. "Primitive" vocalisms in Armstrong's "All of Me" soften sharp body angles, but he sings the lyrics with a proverbial—grammatical, really—wink. "Take my arm, I'll never use them," he promises slyly, which leaves one or two appendages unaccounted for and at the ready, though this is too subtle to be picked up by the run-of-the mill racist sentence-parser. Bigotry persisted in the entertainment business. As late as 1956, Chevrolet, sponsor of *The Dinah Shore Show* on NBC television, wouldn't let her sing a duet with Nat King Cole. At the height of his popularity as a solo act, Cole was more cautious than Armstrong in his frequent choice of silly, unromantic novelties and content-free ballads, such as "Nature Boy" (1948)—Eros denied. The boy in the song, a number-one hit, is in essence a castrato.

When Armstrong was appearing only on "race" records, he didn't have to worry that his evocations of romance and/or sex might be deemed racially offensive. On "I'm Not Rough" (1927), he sings, "I'm crazy about my loving / And I must have it all the time / It takes a brown-skinned woman to satisfy my mind." While these lyrics are broadly amusing in their failure to persuade us he's smooth, the mention of "mind"—the locus of desire and white fear—is surprising and apt. Along with scat, Armstrong's most subtle, prudent, and self-protective ploy with "white" love songs is his interjection of the word "mama" for a recollected, potential, or imagined sexual partner. "Mama" is an endearment reserved for Negro women only in countless blues vocals well into the 1950s. The "mama" usage has a wide emotional and cultural sweep. "Save It, Pretty Mama," Armstrong's "race" record of 1928, is a hymn to chastity, sort of, but the matriarchal, Oedipal, and regressive aspects of this pervasive endearment are no laughing matter; nor is the paternal void it implies. "Oh, mama, mama, mama," Armstrong sings achingly in "Gully Low Blues" (1927), a waif as much as a lover, his lament complementing the wrenching clarinet solos by Johnny Dodds that precede and follow it, Dodds dropping down an octave, gully low, a personification of the emotive small-group style of New Orleans/Chicago jazz—intimate exchanges between equal partners, male or female. When Armstrong interjects "mama" in an erotically alive song, as he does in both "Star Dust" and Carmichael's "Georgia on My Mind" (also 1931), he's subliminally saying that the woman is colored. *"Sweet Mama!"* Armstrong adds at the end of his straightforward rendition of the lyrics to "Exactly Like You" (1930), but only after two beats of silence have passed, as though he's heard a hostile male voice call out from the white audience, "Exactly like who?" "It's only a sweet mama, a brown-skinned gal. No offense," says Armstrong in effect—unsmiling, and naked as such.

"Mask is the key word," says Humbert Humbert, whose rhetorical sleights-of-hand in *Lolita* allow him to get away with every crime. It helps him, too, that almost all the sex is off stage, out of sight, or implied, as it is in Matisse and mainstream Armstrong. The virtues of indirection, understatement, and scat singing are easily demonstrated by comparing Gaston Lachaise's *Torso* (1928) and Matisse's *The Rumanian Blouse* (1940), completed while France was being overwhelmed by Germany and three years before Matisse began his *Jazz* series despite the historic moment. No authoritative scholarly comparison of Lachaise's fragmented, *faux*-ancient *Torso* (figs. 73, 74) with one of its precursors, a fertility amulet of antiquity—the *Venus of Willendorf,* for one (30,000–20,000 B.C.)—could possibly rescue Lachaise's attempt to distill the Female Principle, now a "sexist" idea burdened by feminist theoretical baggage heavier than her extra buttocks and iconographically correct big breasts. Matisse seems to have squeezed her muscle-bound sister into a billboard-flat blouse that at once expresses strength without causing offense or mirth and suggests raw sexuality with its great (vulval?) folds of soft skirt and its red sprouts. She's tanned, by "red weather," to use Wallace Stevens's phrase again, our leitmotif from "Disillusionment of Ten O'Clock," where "The houses are haunted / By white night-gowns. / None are green, / Or purple with green rings, / Or green with yellow rings"—veritable Matisse images to hang in *The Red Studio* (fig. 13) or next to *The Rumanian Blouse.* The asymmetrical tilt of her roomy shoulders subliminally seats her on a capacious, plush red couch. Matisse's title itself telescopes the distancing operation— "blouse" instead of "woman"—just as *Forms,* at the literal midpoint of *Jazz* and World War II, distills the Female Principle and form most austerely, and at a time when Matisse's health was failing badly (fig. 76). Brancusi's *Bird in Space* completes the process of distillation with a miracle of conflation, a divested form that is at once a geyser, a flame, a bird feather, a fish rising, a phallus, and a vulva or labia in textbook silhouette—the high end of euphemistic refinement (fig. 77).

Armstrong, the masked master of obliquity, is especially sly and potent on "Lazy River" (1931), where scat singing "blouses" and covers up naked self-expression. "Lazy River" 's covert eroticism is ideally set off by first listening to Hoagy Carmichael, an Armstrong pal, singing his own lyrics (the melody is by Sidney Arodin) in 1930, a year before Armstrong's version. Carmichael's "Lazy River," recorded under his own name, posits a worry-proof Currier and Ives pastoral—with cookie-cutter lyrics such as "old mill run," "noonday sun," "blue skies up above / everyone's in love"—where no one could possibly be making love, to judge by the decorous way Carmichael's recording orchestra of first-rate jazzmen plays it, a celeste chiming properly in the background. But when Armstrong's three saxophones play the melody on his recording, he hits them with mock exhortations every few measures—"yeah," "uh-huh," "*sure!*"—all in a lightly sarcastic tone, a wry self-parody of his customary (sometimes willed) enthusiasm that calls to mind "Laughin' Louie" and suggests he's quite put off by their unsaxy delivery and the bland folkiness of the hokey lyrics he's supposed to sing. There is a limit. "Way down, way down," he says, speaking to himself here—it's too late for those saxophones—announcing where and how he's going to travel.

Armstrong may really mean *down,* with all its vernacular and obscene connotations. "Mama, mam*u-uh,*" Armstrong adds to the lyrics of "Lazy River" before he scats. In "Empty Bed Blues" (1928), a "race" record, Bessie Smith could pine openly for her "coffee-grinder" man and "deep-sea diver" who "can touch the bottom and his wind holds out so long." It would be quite satisfying if some dictionary allowed that *scat* abbreviates "scatological." (Armstrong's selected published letters [1999] reveal him to have been hilariously ribald.) As it is, Carmichael's line "up a lazy river" encourages us to take the low road. "Oh, you *rascal,* you *dog!*" chortles Armstrong self-reflexively during his incomprehensible, "muzzled" scat chorus. Although Nat King Cole sings several lines of "Non Dimenticar (Don't Forget)" (1958) in Italian, his silken delivery doesn't make us yearn for a translation that would unmask any discreetly hidden intimacies.

The sounds Armstrong makes are so unique and beyond translitera-

73. Gaston Lachaise, *Torso,* rear view, 1928. Bronze.

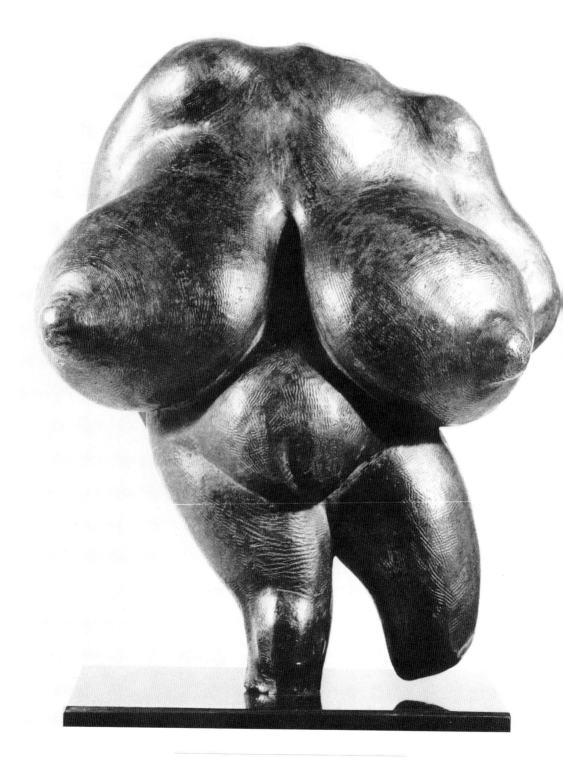

74. Gaston Lachaise, *Torso,* front view, 1928.

75. Henri Matisse, *The Rumanian Blouse*, 1940.

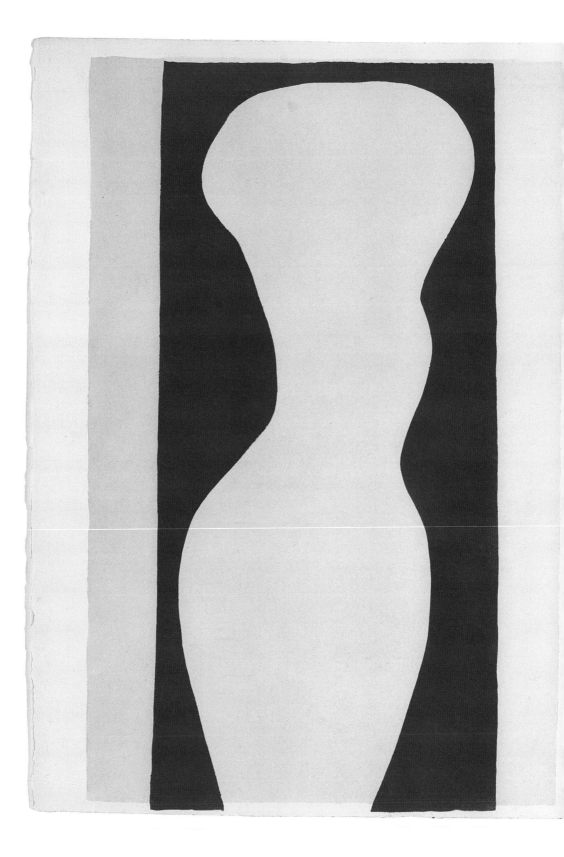

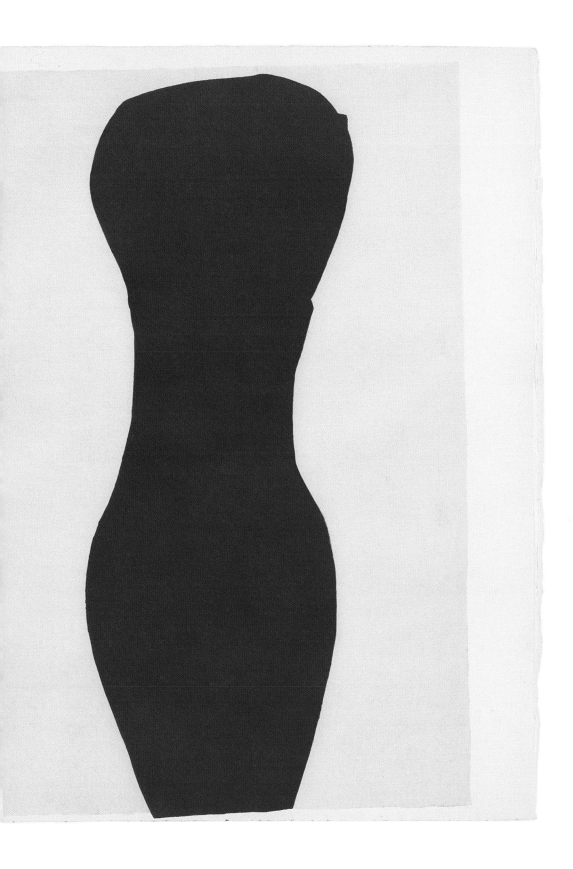

tion that he could be talking to the dogs, birds, or fish. While he is singing "Jeepers Creepers" to the horse in the movie *Going Places,* there's an extraordinary moment when he seems to mesmerize the beast, who stops snorting and tossing its head to listen to Pops sing. Armstrong himself, who often seems to be singing in a (viper's?) trance, ends his "Lazy River" scat with comprehensible words whose rhythmically subtle and sensual flow defies punctuation when transcribed: "Up a lazy river *mmm* river oh you *river* oh you dog! Oh you *river!* Look out, Charlie Alexander," he says, surfacing from his body of water (Alexander's piano briefly sounds). Armstrong the "signifying" trickster is deeply amused that no one has understood his transgressive private language(s)—no one until now, that is, though we are not rushing to print it here. His scat skirts obscenity the way Matisse's *The Rumanian Blouse* clothes Lachaise's *Torso* (figs. 73, 75) and Joyce, conversely, lifts the lid near the end of *Ulysses:* "if he wants to kiss my bottom Ill drag open my drawers and bulge it right out in his face as large as life if he can stick his tongue 7 miles up my hole," thinks Molly Bloom (*Ulysses,* page 780). Ladies and gentlemen, now you know why scat was invented.

Unlike Armstrong, Waller the performer is King Leer on sexual matters, a most imprudent colored man. Andy Razaf's lyrics for Waller's "Honeysuckle Rose" eroticize the flower, in the direction of Georgia O'Keeffe's vaginal and vulval blooms: "Don't buy sugar / You just have to touch my cup," sings Waller in a light comic tone, briefly playing the part of the flower addressing Waller the pollinating "honey bee." "You're my sugar . . . / It's sweet when you stir it up / *Honeysuckle rose,*" and he drops his voice singing the final two words, showing mock reverence for the wondrous forces of nature. His pianism is peppy rather than "sexy," but the band's lilting riff, taken at a below medium tempo, is very insinuating. (This is the 1934 recording of their 1929 song.) The horns don't solo, a rare occurrence, allowing the riffs to constitute a sweet and slow ride down a lazy river of Waller's making—eleven choruses, more than twice the usual number. "Yes, yes," he booms at the end. The unintentional echo of Molly Bloom's famous words is appropriate if you allow synesthesia here: the riffs sound and move like

Molly, whose concluding stream-of-consciousness is syncopated prose. In "I'm Gonna Sit Right Down and Write Myself a Letter" (1935), Waller sings that in addition to words on the page, there will be "a lot of kisses on the bottom," which may bring to mind Leopold Bloom. Another Waller double entendre won't hold up if you don't know old slang or that apartment buildings had coal-burning stoves and furnaces. "No, lady, we can't haul your ashes for twenty-five cents. That's bad business," he quips, outrageously, at the end of "Spring Cleaning (Getting Ready for Love)" ("hauling ashes" is also sexual intercourse). The song titles "Sweet and Slow" (1935) and "Hold Tight" (1939) are double entendres that call for no scholia unless you think the second title refers to a woman's arms alone. Sexually droll Miró often "scats" in visual double entendre, a private (parts) language where forms hold tight (fig. 81). It is inconceivable that Armstrong, raised in the South, could have let loose like New Yorker Waller, or allowed himself to be photographed dancing with a young white woman, even in international waters (fig. 20).

"Turn out de lights and call de law!" Waller shouts at the end of another record, when his band is really cookin' and he fears that everything will fly out of control. Police sirens and whistles sound on the record, as in "The Joint Is Jumpin' " (1937), two bursts of aleatory music after the example of Varèse or Waller's friend Gershwin, who includes auto horns in the score of *An American in Paris* (1928). Waller's dialectical turns on *the* and *de law* parody the darky entertainer's self-protective masks at the same time that Waller is sustaining and hiding behind another large comic person/persona—the buffoonish fat man. Double entendres and leers notwithstanding, no one is going to take this 280-pound Negro seriously as a romantic figure, broad pun intended. Our grandmothers were safe, and we're still drawing on his body of work.

By the 1950s, *his* fifties, Armstrong was fervently singing romantic songs from the perspective of banked fires, his reduced vocal range expressive in the manner of Walter Huston's delivery of "September Song" (1938). As for the younger, more vital men of color who aspired to the Crosby-Sinatra mantle, the politic Nat King Cole only dared to address directly a long-dead white woman of good family ("Mona Lisa," the number-one hit of 1950), while the baritone Billy Eckstine, the "breakthrough" black balladeer, was crooning to seduce our sisters, sweethearts, aunts, and mothers. "Taking a Chance on Love," Eckstine sang in 1951, a policy Armstrong had avoided as a performer, and now, it seemed, as a man. "(When We Are Dancin') I Get Ideas," also from 1951, is suggestive enough, but Armstrong's muted opening trumpet solo and concluding improvisation are surprisingly soulful— too restrained to convince us that the fifty-year-old musician is eager to act on any erotic "ideas," easy sweet mamas notwithstanding.

"I Get Ideas" represents Armstrong's awkward and precarious position in the musical culture of the early 1950s, when he tried to please two constituencies. His All Stars (a sextet) were pitted against the jazz new wave of bebop musicians ("That's what I call jujitsu music," he said in 1954), while his record company, Decca, and manager, Joe Glaser, also expected him to compete with the top pop singers of the day, however commercial the material. "I Get Ideas" had already been recorded suavely by Tony Martin, to a rousing tango orchestration. Armstrong's comparatively reserved version nonetheless proved popular and established him firmly as a dependable "cover" artist who could make distinctive successful versions of someone else's hit song. This had started with his cover of a Frankie Laine hit, "That Lucky Old Sun" (1949), and other cover recordings followed: "That's My Desire" (Laine again); "La Vie en Rose" (Edith Piaf); "C'est Si Bon (It's So Good)" (Eartha Kitt); "If" (Perry Como); "The Gypsy" (Dinah Shore); and "Kiss of Fire" (Georgia Gibbs, who is the emblem of aggressive showbiz mediocrity in Lenny Bruce's best and longest recorded sketch, "The Palladium," 1959). Even serious students of Armstrong continue to ignore this wide-ranging, market-driven array of songs—unfortunately, since "I Get Ideas" is one of several pieces of fifties fluff transformed by thespian Armstrong into a coherent body of low-expectation love songs, as though the Picasso or Braque of 1912 had collaged a delicate bouquet out of autumn-hued wallpaper remnants.

Armstrong's low-expectation love songs of 1949–52 are more poignant and quietly, unintentionally ironic because he's often backed by the same kind of overwrought orchestral strings and choirs that complemented or enhanced the physical splendor and erotic dynamism of Eckstine. Armstrong doesn't joke or scat much in the music that addresses the fact of his own middle-age and, by implication, waning sexual powers and mortality. He manages to express loneliness without sounding pathetic. The most memorable of his low-expectation songs are "(Give Me) A Kiss to Build a Dream On," on the other side of the "I Get Ideas" 78-rpm disc ("and my imagination will do the rest," he sings); "Blueberry Hill" ("Come climb the hill with me, baby / We'll see what we shall see / I'll bring my horn with me," Armstrong warbles confidently of an imagined reunion with his Eve of long ago); "It's All in the Game," where he's sanguine about a friend's chances at love, as tired as he himself sounds, possibly overwhelmed by Gordon Jenkins's clamorous, Wagnerian arrangement—the musical embodiment of romantic expectations frighteningly amuck, aural Viagra; and "La Vie en Rose," in English, whose unembarrassed, open expressiveness and untranslatable, contra-Piaf optimism ("we'll have la vie en rose," he concludes) are very touching in Sy Oliver's understated arrangements and should be even more affecting and impressive now, fifty years later, to Armstrong devotees who were then a permanent, immortal eighteen, dancing cheek-to-cheek to such Billy Eckstine hits as "I Wanna Be Loved" (1950), or Armstrong's "A Kiss to Build a Dream On," introduced by Armstrong in a forgettable Mickey Rooney movie, *The Strip* (1951), which helped make it a hit record—among *Billboard* magazine's Top Twenty best-sellers for eleven weeks in 1951–52, surprisingly enough, and justly, since the song was a previously unrecorded reject from the 1930s.

"Sweetheart, I ask no more than this / A kiss to build a dream on" is a modest request, less a tribute to romance than a gloss on the male state of mind we currently call "midlife crisis," and long the central subject and motive force of Picasso's art. This is especially true of the years 1927–35, after the forty-six-year-old Picasso had begun an affair with seventeen-year-old Maria-Thérèse Walter. LA BATAILLE S'EST ENGAGÉ reads the bottom line in his 1912 collage (fig. 8). "Was he up for this one?" is the vulgar question. *Figures by the Sea* ("January 2, 1932," he dated the back of the canvas) is one answer, evidence of the fifty-one-year-old artist's horrible fears of sexual failure—"I get ideas" indeed (fig. 80). This is literally a far cry from the nude produced and visually possessed by Picasso the one-man rhythm section of 1908 (fig. 33). His extroverted wallpaper and exquisitely balanced collage of 1912 looks like even sweeter music now. Viewers ordinarily repelled by Picasso's violent and bizarre distortions of the female form should find the humanity of this beach scene most compelling because his male and female subjects suffer the crisis together as equal partners in a kiss that is already a bad dream—a scream, in fact. Their Blueberry Hill is a beach cabana, recognized by any French person of style as a trysting site. This one, however, has turned to stone, along with everything else, the two figures cast in a testicular form that mocks the ancient phallic altar of Dionysius at Delos and Picasso's capacities as a lover. He may also be sending up Eve-empowering Brancusi (fig. 31), whose

78. "September Song": Rabbit Maranville, age 41, Boston Braves, spring training, 1931.

79. "It's All in the Game": Big Sid Catlett, New York City, c. 1943. Photographed by William P. Gottlieb.

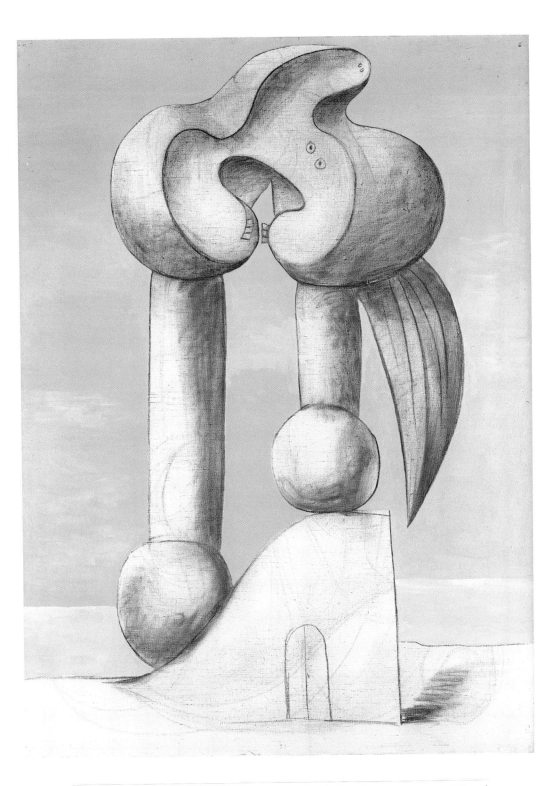

80. "Blueberry Hill": Pablo Picasso, *Figures by the Sea,* January 2, 1932. Oil and charcoal on canvas.

81. "I Wanna Be Loved": Joan Miró, *Young Woman in a Hat*, 1936.

82. "La Vie en Rose": Henri Matisse, *Red Interior: Still Life on a Blue Table,* 1947.

83. "What a Wonderful World": Constantin Brancusi, *The Newborn II,* marble version, 1920, photographed by Brancusi. The weathered or time-ravaged "primordial" wood used by Brancusi for his pedestals was salvaged from torn-down old Parisian buildings. This base was first exhibited in 1926—a new composition from old cords. It's Jazz Aged in design. What music was he listening to?

84. Jack Teagarden singing, c. 1953, adjusting his ear just so, it would seem, as befits Apollinaire's antennae in the flesh. William P. Gottlieb, the photographer, has shot from a Léger-informed position, emphasizing the "crane" in the foreground—technology and music as a constructive presence, metal sculpture by Picasso, too, titled *Profile of Girl with Pony Tail.*

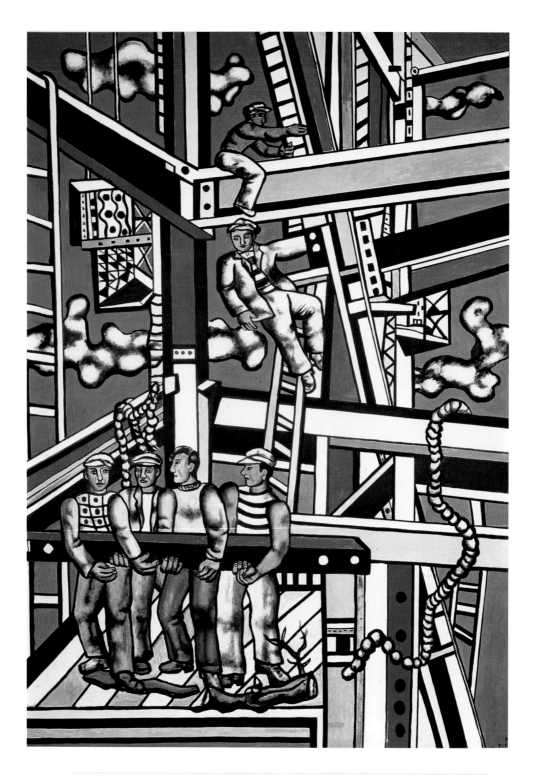

85. Fernand Léger, *The Constructors*, 1950. The self-conscious posing begs for symbolic readings unless the workers have spotted a photographer on a nearby structure.

86. Marc Riboud, *Eiffel Tower*, 1954. The painter, a Léger-trained construction-ist, is undaunted by the ways the Tower, international symbol of technological prowess and the bliss of altitude, has been compromised already by tourism and kitsch (e.g., Eiffel Tower pencil sharpeners and thermometers).

euphoria and perfectionism (fig. 77) he detested as being too far from experience—sentimental in its almost programmatic affirmation of existence, including the Genesis lighting of Brancusi's photographs of his own work (fig. 83). Picasso deems sexual dysfunction so grotesque and regressive that the Siamese-twin-like lovers must also endure identical baby teeth and the same swooning cartoon ghost phallic nose, Picasso drawing upon an old configuration alive even today in the comic book *Casper the Friendly Ghost* (b. 1949).

By precisely dating his pictures, especially after 1926, Picasso the relentlessly candid diary-keeper lets us see that he typically spent only two days on each open revelation—no scat here—painting up-tempo continuously, it seems, day and night, like a frantic, aging jazz improviser who would welcome the support of a tireless drummer. Several of his greatest and most famous paintings were whipped out this quickly in 1932 alone, in the wake of the sketchy *Figures by the Sea* (January 2): *The Dream* (January 24); *Woman in a Red Armchair* (January 27); *The Mirror* (March 12); *Girl Before a Mirror* (March 14). Jo Jones has already been spelled here by Big Sid Catlett, who, depressed and exhausted by the pictures, pauses while Picasso stops to choose a broader brush (fig. 79). "Man, bring out ol' Matisse to paint 'Honeysuckle Rose'," thinks Catlett, who will soon be replaced by Buddy Rich and then Louie Bellson. My remarks on *Figures by the Sea* demonstrate what happens if an average senior citizen lets himself ruminate on several sad or rueful phrases in Armstrong. A "literary" mind notes that Armstrong doesn't get to play his instrument on Blueberry Hill. "No roominate in sight," Fats Waller might have punned at the end of one of these songs about the romantically challenged.

"*C'est si bon . . .* I say it like the French people do," Armstrong also sang in 1950, with the uncomplicated erotic brio we expect of Picasso's friends Miró and Matisse as opposed to the coyness of Eartha Kitt on her version. Miró, the forty-three-year-old cartoonist of *Young Woman in a Hat* (1936), employs a witty light touch where Picasso petrifies, Miró mixing actual sand into the yellow pigments of the woman's hourglass figure (fig. 81). The X-ray vision of Miró's male gaze penetrates the

OPPOSITE: 87. Brassaï, *The Eiffel Tower, View from the Gates of the Trocadéro,* 1931–32. To light up the Tower like anyone's Christmas tree is to bring its symbolism home or reduce the Tower to another kitschy tourist souvenir. Its toylike scale, determined by the gates and previous images, underscores the effect.

black to reveal a phallic red cranium. It's on her mind, it *is* her mind. She clearly wants her ashes hauled. Has Fats Waller taken up painting? But Miró is more pro-life than vaingloriously phallocentric: the hat is at once an egg that spermatozoa can't miss and a womb, and they are taking off at a forty-five-degree angle, celebrating the idea of conception rather than carnal pleasure, or so it seems. Only serious students of Miró and the secret language of scat will recognize her spidery dark eyes as a variant of Miró's customary iconographic depiction of the vagina, vulva, and pubic hair. The hole below them is—"Enough! Enough!" yells a decorous young mother. The womb-hat evokes art history as well as new life (fig. 81). Onetime students of the facts of life who remember the schematic drawings in biology texts of spermatozoa rushing toward eggs should recognize seventy-eight-year-old Matisse's D-Day assault in *Red Interior: Still Life on a Blue Table* (1947)—no lazy river, this. The symbolism is oblique enough to say that if this were another Armstrong number, he has safely scatted around dangerous waters once again, even as major-league baseball was about to be integrated. By 1963, however, Armstrong could sing familiarly, "Hello, Dolly! This is Louis, Dolly," a famous opening line that signaled on several levels that it was no longer sleepy time down South.

Everyone seemed to know Louis by 1964, when his record of "Hello, Dolly!" displaced a Beatles song as number one on the *Billboard* sales chart; he even managed to upstage Barbra Streisand in his brief appearance in the 1969 film version of the show. To translate Matisse's *The Nightmare of the White Elephant* (from *Jazz*) into quite arbitrary racial terms, Armstrong is the flight of black arabesques whirling around the spectral beast (fig. 69). Armstrong's concluding trumpet solo on "Hello, Dolly!" is a model of melodic improvisation—hardly a confirmation of a commercial "sell-out." During the last two decades of his life (he died in 1971), Armstrong was a public figure, the only person in the jazz world who criticized President Dwight D. Eisenhower for not offering verbal support to the black children who integrated Central High School in Little Rock, Arkansas, in 1957—hardly the act of an Uncle Tom. Armstrong appeared on the covers of *Time* (1949) and *LIFE* (1966), was interviewed on television by Edward R. Murrow, and toured the world with his All Stars as "Ambassador Satch," sometimes with State Department sponsorship.

This celebrity and the predictability in the 1960s of his music and his ebullience made him old-hat and Uncle Tom still to many serious people, especially those unsmiling young African-Americans who today, as academic scholars and teachers, should be rushing to get Armstrong and Ellington into the Afro-American and "diversified" curricula ahead of, say, the estimable Langston Hughes, who is now on everyone's reading list and featured in anthologies. Although Armstrong's All Stars deteriorated, like the trumpeter's health, after 1965, the All Stars of the 1950s produced much excellent music. Their first-rate LP tribute to Waller, *Satch Plays Fats* (1955), concludes with a version of "Black and Blue" even more impassioned than the first one (logically so, with the passing of almost thirty more years of racism). The reprise of "Ain't Misbehavin' " repeats the quotation from *Rhapsody in Blue*—musical integration, at the very least. Armstrong and Ella Fitzgerald recorded a *Porgy and Bess* album in 1957, Louis blithely playing the good *and* evil characters—"It's all music, man," as Charlie Parker had said, accepting the "Afro-Cuban" tag. Armstrong's All Stars was in fact always integrated, in all its editions (1947–71), thereby complementing the Civil Rights movement. Ambassador indeed! The social history and importance of jazz integration has never been properly appreciated.

Nor has any art historian noted that Léger, a man of the Left, integrated the absolutely segregated French building industry in his *The Constructors* (1950). At a time when male immigrants of color from any one of the colonies (Algeria to Cameroon to Tahiti) were typically sweeping streets, Léger has placed a brown man (race is also varied chroma) at the top, directing everything, it seems, including the dancing ropes and color-coordinated beams—if anyone can accept the way-out idea of such careful high-wire acts of painting (fig. 85). Growth is symbolized by the unexpected tree branch. *Marshall Plan Boogie Woogie* it could be retitled, a tribute to postwar reconstruction, Léger's good friend Mondrian, and both artists' happy wartime stays in America, whose more open society was esteemed by the democratic Léger. From 1935 to 1939, Léger had painted a 7′ 5″ × 10′ 7″ Polynesian *Adam and Eve*—an act of monumental pan-racialism whose good intentions are underscored by two brown-hued humanoid clouds.

Armstrong's All Stars was the first black band to feature a white musician, Jack Teagarden; Charlie Parker followed with Red Rodney in 1948 (fig. 36). Teagarden happened to have played on Armstrong's first integrated record, "Knockin' a Jug" (1929), and on Fats Waller's, too, where they sang together (1931). Publicity posters of Armstrong and Teagarden from the thirties and forties often picture them as Kings of the Trumpet and Trombone respectively, cartooned crowns atop their heads, and this wasn't hyperbole; each was the premier player on his horn, *King of Kings* in Brancusi's title. The All Stars, a perfect setting for their talents, developed out of a successful but ad-hoc concert engagement held in New York's Town Hall, May 17, 1947, a month after a more celebrated metropolitan act of integration: Jackie Robinson's first major-league game with the Brooklyn Dodgers on April 15, 1947, which broke the color barrier in baseball. Teagarden, who had just given up his debt-ridden big band, fell in quite naturally with Armstrong, who couldn't have found a more suitable partner, black or white. "Looks like you can read my mind," as Teagarden sings to Waller on "That's What I Like About You" (1931), and he could have said the same to Armstrong, or to Big Sid Catlett, the drummer in the first All Stars.

Teagarden the singer epitomizes multicultural jazz music and the modernist impulse to turn dross to brass, as he does with these negligible songs: "I Hope Gabriel Likes My Music" (1936, with Frankie Trumbauer's Orchestra), the brass player's prayer, which Armstrong recorded first; "Stars Fell on Alabama" (1933, and many later versions), where Mitchell Parish would rhyme "Alabama," "hammer," and "glamour"; "A Hundred Years from Today" (1933), where the pressing earnestness of his light baritone voice turns banalities—"Don't save your kisses / Pass them around"—into a *carpe diem* philosophy, almost; and "Love Me" (1933), which is Armstrong-like in the way that Teagarden makes its unvarnished lyrics ring true. "You're all that I desire, love me," is affecting, like Walker Evans' 1936 photo of a plain wooden one-story storefront in Tennessee that bears a crudely hand-lettered sign, CHURCH OF THE NAZARENE / WELCOME. On "Texas Tea Party" (1933, with Benny Goodman's Orchestra), Teagarden sings "Mama mama mama" with perfectly colored but slightly exaggerated angst— one "mama" too many. "Where did you hide my tea?" he laments. The pun on his nickname includes another musician's idiom for marijuana.

Mis'ry isn't amusing on "I Gotta Right to Sing the Blues" (1934), which is one of Teagarden's classic vocals and a petition to be accepted as a soul singer, race notwithstanding: the songwriters, Ted Koehler and Harold Arlen, were white, that's granted, and the composition, technically speaking, isn't a twelve-bar blues, but the loosely held noun "blues" belongs to the psychological vernacular, on multicultural ground. No one seems to notice, or object, that Arlen's "Blues in the Night" (1941), sung originally by a Negro convict in a movie, begins in Black English: "My mama done tol' me . . ." (lyrics by Johnny Mercer). Teagarden, the finest white blues singer, once acknowledged that he'd listened closely to Bessie Smith in the twenties. Her spare use of vibrato and expressive vowel distortions were not lost on Teagarden, who extended and refined these blues basics. On his beautiful and moving 1941 recording of the Negro spiritual "Nobody Knows the Trouble I've Seen," he varies the vowel enunciation of "seen," "hallelujah," and "Lord" each of the three times he sings them, in subtle ways quite beyond Bessie Smith, who was all thunder and steady rain. "Lorhuhu-d," he sings, a phrase that could be played on his trombone. His smeared consonants and lazy behind-the-beat delivery go with his instrument and territory—Texas. On composer-lyricist Johnny Mercer's deceptively jaunty "I'm an Old Cowhand" (1936), Teagarden sings and scats wryly, the jazz soloist in good spirits. But Mercer's surprisingly matter-of-fact, defeatist conclusion—"Look out, Texas, here I come / Right back where I started from"—is particularly wrenching, given Teagarden's death in 1964, age fifty-nine, worn down by ill health, alcoholism, and the failure of so many of his own bands.

When Teagarden first visited New York in 1927 and jammed triumphantly in Harlem, the uptown crowd said he must have some black blood in him. He said no, his heritage was German, of all things, but his empathy, his identification with African-Americans, seems to have been absolutely natural and complete. On "Fare-Thee-Well to Harlem" and "Ol' Pappy" (both 1934) he sings, without dialect, as black men who, by turns, are disillusioned with urban life or duty-bound to return home, though guitarist Nappy Lamare mars each record with his minstrel-show patois. But no one intrudes on Teagarden's startling 1941 version of the Razaf-Waller "Black and Blue." What other Caucasian could or would have sung "Black and Blue," the great racial lament and protest? (Teagarden had shortly before [1940] recorded a rousing instrumental version of "Shine" with a great integrated group—Dave Tough, and, from the Ellington band, Rex Stewart, Ben Webster, and Barney Bigard—without uttering a word of the stereotypical lyrics.) "All my life through / I've been so black and blue," he sings on his 1941 recording. He continues forthrightly, without a hint of self-consciousness or minstrelsy condescension: "I'm white inside / But that don't help my case / Still I can't hide / What's on my face," Teagarden sings, repeating the last phrase urgently, "On my face, Lord"— stretching the vowel on "Lord," an interpolation that makes the song sound like a Negro spiritual, several of which Teagarden recorded in the 1950s. On "Aunt Hagar's Children's Blues" (1956), he says, "I'll let the congregation join"—slipped in straightforwardly where Armstrong and Waller would have played it for laughs as quickly as Teagarden's raffish friends and sometime recording mates Bing Crosby and Johnny Mercer. Like the Brancusi who carved *King of Kings*, Teagarden seems to have forgotten he's white, and so does Armstrong when Tea is beside him on the bandstand. "Yeah, homes," he murmurs to Jack, who's about to solo on a blues at a 1951 concert. ("Homes" is a variant, then and now, for the black vernacular designation of a guy from the neighborhood or hometown.) He addresses Teagarden variously as "Brother Jackson," "boy," and "Daddy," familiarities he extends elsewhere to Negroes alone, though, strikingly, never to the bona fide blacks in the first, best edition of the All Stars (1947–51), none of whom calls Armstrong "papa," as Teagarden does.

Armstrong even seems to anoint Teagarden as an honorary African-American at the May 17, 1947, concert—we should celebrate the anniversary annually as Jack Teagarden Robinson Day—when he underscores the importance of their meeting as equals by having Teagarden play and sing "St. James Infirmary," long one of Armstrong's signature blues, first recorded by him in 1928. "Let her go," Teagarden sings of a dead love stretched out "so cold, so still, so fair" on a slab at St. James, his voice so constricted that the words barely get out. "Let her go, God bless her, wherever she may be-*ea*," and the audible catch in his throat may constrict our throats, too. He completes the blues with his inimitable laconic soulfulness—Afro-Cowhand, it could be labeled to attract more educators to the idea of jazz multiculturism. "I'm in heaven," Teagarden says humbly after the next number, "Royal Garden Blues."

Teagarden's closing "trombone" chorus on "St. James Infirmary" is aleatory music, modernism by definition, though to him it was a proven crowd-pleasing vaudeville trick: using a water glass in place of the trombone's chamber and flared bell, which produced an ethereal, plaintive sound—and here, in the infirmary, some rasping, ascending and descending buzzes, the anguished inner voice of a mourner. Teagarden concludes with eight successively lower and lower single notes, eight steps down into a dark cellar—the wine cellar, given the mood. His lowest blue note—almost a bleat—is hardly low because his bravura, virtuoso handling of the glass constitutes a full cup. It runneth over. "Yeah!" says someone in the audience, and there's a ripple of laughter. Teagarden's calm, relaxed instrumental command implies that nothing can keep him down. His control of low notes represents a figurative high.

"I Can't Give You Anything but Love" (1929) marks another height, the turning point in Armstrong's entire career: his first featured performance of a song by white Tin Pan Alley tunesmiths, the redoubtable Broadway/Hollywood team of Dorothy Fields and Jimmy McHugh. The enormous commercial and critical success of the number, one of his last releases in OKeh's "race" series, turned Armstrong into a mainstream performer and established the big band format and formula he would follow until he returned to a combo in 1947. The distinction and artistic success of "I Can't Give You Anything but Love" hinges on the way Armstrong manages to tell a story on two levels about the doubts and hesitations experienced by a woman's suitor—an ordinary guy—and, simultaneously, the deep fears of a second fellow, little Louis, "Laughin' Louie," the ambitious colored boy from back o' town who will pull out all stops to conquer the world. Although the slangy number is customarily sung in a cocky, James Cagney tough-tender manner, Armstrong opens his version with a timorous, muted trumpet statement that, after only half a chorus, he uncharacteristically passes on to his excellent trombonist, J. C. Higginbotham, who sounds especially robust following Armstrong as he completes the half-cooked melodic chorus with a sweeping, out-of-tempo flourish. Armstrong then begins to sing the unchallenging lyrics with some physical difficulty, it seems—breathlessly, as though he were walking up a hill or is on the brink of hyperventilation. The plucky message of the title lyric, "I can't give you anything but love, baby," kept the song popular throughout the Depression, but a thick-tongued Armstrong hesitates for a heartbeat or two before and after he has to emit the newly difficult words ". . . love . . . baby . . ."—and he does this twice, with considerable force, biting off the word "baby," which is always sung with a sustained open vowel. It's as though he's thinking, Does she even want me? And if she does, will I be up to it? Physiologically, he's singing from a dry well. Who hasn't been there? The gray ceiling above our empty conjugal bed. The arctic white ceiling above the hospital bed. Am I awake or dreaming? This Armstrong, the great actor who taught Billie Holiday and Frank Sinatra how to dramatize a mere thirty-two-bar song (listen to Sinatra's 1958 "One for My Baby"), posits the essence of the modernist enterprise because his act of imaginative transformation wrests or wrings so much from so little. Suddenly Armstrong's spine stiffens, and in a vocal version of one of his stop-time trumpet choruses, he momentarily halts the rhythm and uneven horizontal flow of the lyrics and emphatically articulates separate words and short phrases from the song, lopping them off the suspended line—"Gee, I'd like to see you looking good, baby"—as he moves from left to right, chopping away, letting the solid shards fall, one atop another, in a vertical column in space, if you will, a spinal chord that manages to double the song's baby population:

GEE!

I'D LIKE TO!

SEE YA!

LOOKIN'!

SWELL!

BU-BA-A-BEE!

BAY-BUH-LOO!

The two Armstrongs of the story have come together and are standing tall and holding their ground—in retrospect a thrilling moment in Armstrong's life and art, the genesis of his great international career. He is figuratively standing next to any one of several strong Brancusi vertical structures—*Adam and Eve,* say, whose wood is by definition organic and vulnerable, evidenced especially by the little cracks and flaws in Adam (fig. 31). Adam's coiled Africanesque energies are about to spring, and Eve is man enough to handle anything, as we can see. "I *can* give you love," Armstrong has been saying in effect all along, "and be an international star of stage, screen, and radio." Armstrong was in fact the first black performer to have a regular radio show, in 1937, sponsored by Fleischmann's Yeast, another leavening force. In turn, there were three Armstrong 78s in Brancusi's record collection, including the bravura "New Tiger Rag" (1932).

Buoyed by new or regained confidence after his "vertical" burst, Armstrong completes the lyric with authority and plays a stately, slowly developed solo that rises, dips, traces rolling hills, includes a stop-time break to parallel the vertical vocal, and climbs quickly, topped by six or seven high, fast, penetrating notes—brassy, happy coitus, one would like to say, but the final three notes are rather flat and unpleasant, as though the highest geometric form in one of Malevich's images of ascending planes were tipped over and caught in a downdraft (fig. 96), which for Armstrong means a moment of self-doubt on his first solo flight with pure white material. For supreme sonic success, listen to Armstrong's solo on "Swing That Music" (1936).

Taken at Armstrong's fastest tempo ever, an astonishing three hun-

88. H. Blancard, *Untitled* (construction of the Eiffel Tower), February 1888. If this and the following images of the Eiffel Tower going up were stills or a montage in a Ken Burns documentary film titled *Flight,* the soundtrack might well emit Armstrong's "New Tiger Rag," an exercise in speed—eight flashy choruses, the trumpeter announcing the number of each successive chorus as he gets to it ("seven . . . eight . . ."), like a countdown for a NASA lift-off or the completion of the Eiffel Tower.

89. H. Blancard, *Untitled* (Eiffel Tower), June 1888.

90. H. Blancard, *Untitled* (Eiffel Tower), August 1888.

91. H. Blancard, *Untitled* (Eiffel Tower), April 28, 1889.

dred beats per minute on the metronome, "Swing That Music" is well named: only a computer or an EKG could possibly calibrate and transcribe the way Armstrong's teeming minuscule rhythmic inflections variously fall on or just off the basic metric pulse. (Only Charlie Parker's "Koko" is faster.) After singing the spirited but innocuous vocal of "Swing That Music," Armstrong plays four choruses, twice his customary number, and they constitute his most technically phenomenal solo ever, a classic in the trumpet canon. It ends with fifty stabbing, single high Cs climaxed by an E-flat as though Brancusi's Adam and Eve were jetting off for their honeymoon on Air Malevich (fig. 96) or one of Brancusi's huge, sawtoothed, rocketlike roosters. On a musical curve, *Bird in Space* can top high C easily (fig. 77). If fellow trumpeters were visible in the audience when he played "Swing That Music" or "New Tiger Rag," Armstrong the competitor would conclude with one hundred high Cs and a high F—a bird or plane in outer space, the tiger by the tail.

The trumpet has lately been called a "phallocentric" instrument, and the high notes of "Swing That Music" have always been criticized as mere showing off, even by Armstrong's admirers. It *is* malevaunting, of a harmless sort, in better taste than Harleys and muscleshirts and of considerable interest given the continued appeal of such music. High-note trumpeting conceivably thrills some listeners even now as the aural equivalent of risky flying, of the highs of altitudes—physical and/or metaphysical—celebrated earlier in the century by almost any image of the Eiffel Tower; the sleek aerodynamic design of every sort of industrial product; the mass adulation of daring aviators from Charles Lindbergh and Amelia Earhart to comic-strip pilots such as Captain Easy, Tailspin Tommy, Barney Baxter, Scorchy Smith, and Smilin' Jack; cross-country races and national air shows featuring spectacular stunts; and by modernist painters such as Malevich, Charles Sheeler, Roger de la Fresnaye, and Robert Delaunay, especially Delaunay's cloud-bursting Eiffel Tower paintings and *Homage to Blériot,* the French pilot (1914). Here, a gravity-defiant dragonfly of a biplane rises to the top edge and almost out of the picture at an unlikely ninety-degree angle, an exaggeration of the thrilling photos of ascending planes that were featured in the international picture press through the 1930s, before total war compromised the romance of flight. NASA renewed it briefly. "Everything was striving to leave the globe, and to make its way further into space," wrote the mystical Malevich in 1919. "The pilot conducts an unending war with his aeroplane [read trum-

92. Walker Evans, *Sidewalk and Shopfront,* New Orleans, 1935.

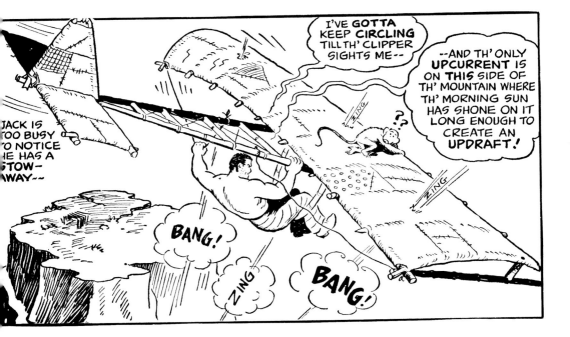

93. Zack Mosley, a frame from his comic strip *Smilin' Jack,* March 5, 1939, in which Jack tries to escape from the Death Island Penal Colony.

94. Levitatin' Louie: Jim Flora, album cover, 1947. The commercial artist Flora has assimilated several aspects of modernism. The partly black piano reflects the buoyant blacks of Matisse, Miró, Léger, Malevich, and Stuart Davis. The flat sepia hues of Armstrong's skin, the banjo, clarinet bell, piano trimming, and HOT-titled pennant would reduce or remove the issue of race. Color becomes a matter of pure play, the domain of Matisse, Derain, Dufy, and Delaunay. Armstrong's name atop the album cover is composed in the manner and spirit of modernist collage, Flora varying five or six typefaces with a jazz improviser's sense of glee—specifically the half-valving and squeezed notes of Ellingtonians Rex Stewart and Clark Terry—Flora here laying out a *Diminuendo in Typeface* (as Ellington would title it) if you follow the lettering of Armstrong's high-flying name from left to right.

pet}; he wants to overcome it and to graft onto himself this new grown body, to fuse it inseparably with his organism."

If the space-flight argument doesn't justify Armstrong's high-note trumpeting, then perhaps it's at least feasible to call it the *élan vital* and halt here—in midair, with Jim Flora's 1947 vision of the *élan vital* (fig. 94)—acceptable Negro levitation (unlike Josephine Baker's, fig. 19), jazz in pre-Sputnik orbit. A grounded Walker Evans rose to proverbial heights in 1935 by discovering a humble, windowless barbershop in New Orleans whose decorator has turned it into a zebra that complements the hand-painted barber pole—jazzlike improvisations or riffs on the standard commercial barbershop motif, public art in place of dull glass. The barber pole also turns out to be public art, a pedestal displaying a local folk limner's version of Brancusi's *Bird in Space* (fig. 77). Coincidence or design has placed in the doorway a woman whose matching striped blouse proves that the universe is an ordered space, from the bottom notes to high F. PERFECTO, reads the sign on the right, boosted by oblique-angled stripes, a zebra taking off (fig. 92). Carlo Carrà's *Free-Word Painting (Patriotic Celebration)* offers the view from space, from the cockpit of a high F (fig. 98) or, more credibly, Flora's Levitatin' Louie (fig. 94).

Armstrong really did embody the life force, viscerally and literally, as I saw in June 1955 when Armstrong and his All Stars were appearing at the Broadway jazz club Basin Street East. Its unusually high stage (the same level as a strip-tease joint) projected well into the audience, which created the possibility of a theater-in-the-round feeling. Armstrong naturally tried to realize this potential intimacy by having the four mobile members of the band play at least one of their forty-five-minute sets of music while facing each of the three sides of the room, which of course forced Armstrong to play with his back to one part of the audience, and then in profile. This afforded startling new views from front-row seats of Armstrong in action, just above us: stocky, not tall, his feet planted firmly on the stage, fourteen or so inches apart on an up-tempo number, knees slightly bent and locked in place tightly like a street laborer manning a jackhammer, his calves vibrating rapidly against his trousers in time with the vibrato of his round, swelling brass sound. Armstrong, we could see, played the trumpet with his entire body—"body and SOUL," you say, and if you rushed to reassemble and interpolate the song title the way any self-respecting collagist would, you're still a modernist, even after the millennium. Evidently you've forgotten postmodernism, which of course retired the concept of *soul*.

Armstrong's famous lambent smile, produced night after night for
fifty years, may have become a rictus—"Laughin' Louie"'s reflex
action—as fixed and false as the teeth in Covarrubias's *Vanity Fair*
"Impossible Interview" (fig. 17). But it's still warming, wherever it's
reproduced, like the saturated red or yellow skies in Matisse and the
subliminal, serious sunrise in the upper right corner of the Covarrubias.
The caption under Covarrubias in the original *Vanity Fair* concludes
with Kreisler about to play "Nagasaki" on the violin and accept Armstrong's invitation to join the band, and this "impossible" multicultural union is already working visually: Kreisler's hair and mustache
got rhythm while his sharp, flat geometric profile is up-to-date. This
thoroughly modern form defines one of several spatial arrowheads that
reinforce the sense of their kinetic energy and Armstrong's (sun)rising
spirits. "Babe, when you laughin', the sun comes shinin' through," he
sings in "When You're Smiling" (1929). In the final decade of his life,
Armstrong would play a tape of this song backstage to inspire him
before a performance whenever he was feeling particularly depleted or
even depressed. How startling it is to come upon an unposed photo of
Armstrong in unsmiling repose (fig. 97). "Stay alive!" he tells the band,
off-mike, at a 1951 concert after they've played "You Can Depend on
Me" and he's ready to sail into the next number and deliver the goods.
When, in 1965, I met Armstrong backstage after the All Stars had

OPPOSITE: 95. The High Hard One—Van Lingle Mungo, pitcher for the
Brooklyn Dodgers, 1936, shot from the worm's-eye angle introduced in Europe
circa 1925 by avant-garde photographers such as Alexander Rodchenko. Mungo's
phallocentric posture passes muster because he led the National League in strike-
outs that year, the only way he could win eighteen games—while absorbing nineteen losses!—in the face of his terrible team's seventh-place finish (out of eight).
"Van Lingle Mungo" is the title of the best baseball song, by the jazz pianist and
singer Dave Frishberg (1969), a multicultural threnody consisting of the recited
names of some forty baseball players from the 1935–50 period. "Heenie Majeski,
Johnny Gee, / Eddie Joost, Johnny Pesky, Thornton Lee, / Danny Gardella, / Van
Lin-gle Mun-go-oh," it begins (for the whole, see Robert Gottlieb and Robert
Kimball's *Reading Lyrics,* 2000). The name of Mungo, who represents the *élan
vital* rather than team play or high finance, is sounded five times with an elegiac
gravity. The song's catalog of names almost scans, as does the lyric "Van Lingle
Mungo"—the basic alternating measures of English (weak, strong / weak,
strong). Mungo defies gravity in the photo.

96. Kasimir Malevich, *Suprematist Composition: Airplane Flying,* 1915.

97. Louis Armstrong, 1961, listening to a playback with Duke Ellington (smiling in the booth).

completed a splendid concert at Stanford University, he was already shirtless, slumped in a camp chair, exhausted, a white bath towel draped over his perspiring torso and another towel wrapped turban-fashion around his head. I was introduced to him as "a professor of English who loves jazz." (Popular culture had no place in the curriculum then, not even soap operas.) Armstrong pretended to misunderstand and, sitting up quickly, did a double take and then held an unblinking look of wide-eyed amazement as he said, *"Professor of Jazz! What this world comin' to?"*

The range and depth of Armstrong's transformative powers are marked by "Sweethearts on Parade," "Just a Gigolo," "Shine," and "Star Dust." Such Armstrong anthology masterpieces as "Potato Head Blues" (1927), "Muggles" (1928), and "West End Blues" (1928) haven't been discussed here because they weren't ragpicker's dross to start with. Even "Star Dust" is tarnished. Mitchell Parish's boilerplate lyrics offer a challenge to the collagist/pasticheur to cut and paste it new, to paraphrase Ezra Pound's call for "fresh dew"—to replicate the kind of Tin Pan Alley trope and rhyme that Ira Gershwin tried to avoid (as in "I Got Rhythm") and Armstrong either raised from the dead or deep-sixed (the kind of vernacular treasured by Gershwin). "Star Dust" ends with the line "the memory of love's refrain," a lyric much beloved and belabored by crooners, repeated twice by Bing Crosby in his 1931 version and three times by Frank Sinatra in his 1940 recording with Tommy Dorsey's big band. But who wants to remember "love's refrain"? And what exactly *is* "love's refrain"? Armstrong drops the entire line—a daring liberty and act of intelligence—and substitutes "Oh, memory, oh, memory, oh, memory," which delighted Hoagy Carmichael. (There are two takes of Armstrong's "Star Dust," and the "memory" variation only appears on the second one, known as the "alternate." Most reissues innocently offer one or the other and make no distinction, with the notable exception of Columbia's *Louis Armstrong / Portrait of the Artist as a Young Man / 1923–1934,* which includes both takes.) Armstrong's startling "oh, memory" interpolation is a plangent apostrophe to the listener to remember his or her own emotions and sensations, which may well be beyond words, certainly beyond Mitchell Parish's imagination and vocabulary. Here we hit the divide that supposedly separates high and low culture and confront nothing less than the limitations of language. James Joyce's sense of those limitations moved him to invent an open-ended punning language for *Finnegans Wake,* where hundreds of American popular songs are included, further evidence that the Irving Berlin Wall has fallen. Who could ask for anything more? An overview, you say?

If we could have levitated above Times Square with Carlo Carrà rather than Mondrian during a War Bond rally in 1942, we might have looked down and imagined a New York vista resembling Carrà's collage *Free-Word Painting (Patriotic Celebration),* though the words would be in English (fig. 98). Although we struggle with the meaning of music, Carrà easily shows how much a picture can say—musically as well as verbally, building upon Picasso's strong start in *Guitar, Sheet Music, and Glass* (fig. 8), the opposite of Rauschenberg's *Monk* (fig. 48). Carrà's collage, whose title asserts the primacy of painting, first appeared as a photomechanical reproduction in the Italian magazine *Lacerba* on August 1, 1914, a few days before Germany and Austria-Hungary declared war on Italy and the Allies. The nationalistic Carrà offers a dynamic aerial view of a pro-war demonstration in a Milan piazza, an exfoliation of doctored newsprint and painted words whose overall design is simultaneously a flower, a wheel, a map, and a sonic record of numerous sounds and sound waves. The concentric circles around the radial center are at once a whirling propeller and a tire, and the quarter moons of black around the hub look like a phonograph record, anticipating the discs subsequently produced by OKeh, Pathé, Bluebird, and Léger.

The title *Free-Word Painting* sounds like an oxymoron, but Carrà does tell us what is going on, in legible verbal tags, headlines, and printed dialogue or "voice-overs." Carrà's name is headline news, bottom far right, and rightly so—his collage is a touchstone for articulate art. Patriotism and aeronautical perspective are fixed at and around the radial center: *ITALIA* ("Italy"); *aviatore* ("aviator"); *eliche perforanti* ("piercing propellers"). In the second ring, white letters against black, the words EEVViiiVAAA iL/REEE ("Lo-o-o-ng Li-i-i-ve the Ki-i-i-ng") and EVVIVAAA/L'ESERCITO ("Lo-o-ng Li-i-i-ve the Army") are jingoistic, and clear enough if you know Italian. The clamor is considerable, our explication very selective. HUHUHUHUHUHUHUH (oblique lettering, off-center, across the black disc or ring) are *sirene* (a plural), as indicated by the almost subliminal lettering spread through it—the sirens of police cars en route to check the collaged tumult and make sure that nothing comes unglued. Carrà posits aleatory music before the fact, without any lessons from Varèse or George Antheil, whose score for the 1924 Léger-Murphy film *Ballet mécanique* includes sirens and gongs. The STRADA/ORCHESTRA (top left, above the musical notes) must be responsible for some of the other onomatopoetic "sounds" that are flying around the *Free-Word Painting,* including, at the center, *rrrrrrraaaaaah urrr*—a car, accelerating and then shifting gears? To its right, at an oblique angle, the screaming effect of AAAAAAaaaaaaaa could be cries in support of war, leading logically to TOT (upper far right, German for "death"), an important note, since it means that Carrà, if not the crowd, isn't celebrating war blindly. Because xenophobic fervor upends reason, the slogans on the two Italian flags are superimposed upside down (bottom left). The patriotism of Mondrian's *Victory Boogie Woogie* is simple, predicated on the fact that three terrible years of war have already passed. SPORTS (beneath the vortex), always fast-breaking news, allows for the most innocent diversions and is complemented by a shard of a scoreboard bearing only zeros, hardly an accidental touch (lower right). Picasso's JOU and BATAILLE cohere admirably.

No one is winning anywhere—an ethical position—except Carrà, whose "headlined" name, typographically reproduced on the lower right, self-reflexively declares that the painter, his conspicuous handmade lettering still in the picture, has, like ragpickers Picasso, Waller, and Armstrong, triumphed over the machine culture by using its output—newsprint or mechanical lyrics—to his advantage. *Salvation* is the operative word. Carrà's concentric circles trace a mandala, the Eastern mystic's symbol of the journey into the mind or soul. The Milan *Daily News* would simply have headlined the story LOCAL ARTIST TAPS SCRAPS AND FRAGMENTS. "Swingin' Them Jingoisms" is Fats Waller's title for Carrà, the collagist who could have done justice to the patriotic raw materials behind *Victory Boogie Woogie.* Carrà's example challenges the official art history opinion that his and Picasso's and Braque's kind of 1912–15 collage—affectionately gathered, delicately arrayed, and legible—lead straight to Pop art, that joyless offshoot of Dadaism, TOT with a wink, or the odd violence of Rauschenberg's war-torn *Monk* (fig. 48). Modernism may have ended historically around 1965, with the apotheosis of both Pops. Carrà the painter celebrates his rescue operation with two drum rolls, transliterated and printed along the bottom to the left of his name: TRrrrrrrrrrrrr and TRRRRRR. Jo Jones picks them up in the wings and raises the volume, a smooth and seamless interactive segue that marks Carrà's collage as cutting-edge jazz modernism.

98. Carlo Carrà, *Free-Word Painting (Patriotic Celebration)*, 1914. Pasted papers, newsprint, and gouache on cloth, mounted on wood.

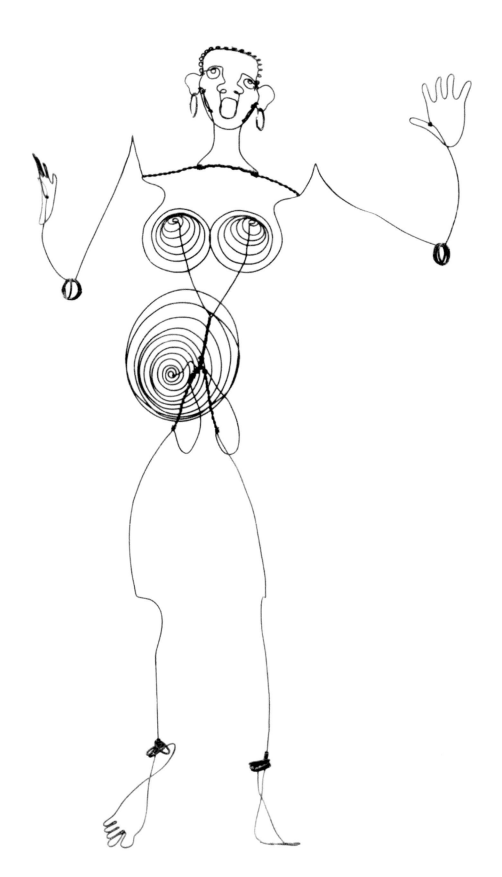

4

Joys for Everyone

The anonymous publicist who advertised Armstrong in 1932 as "Master of Modernism" probably didn't grasp the accuracy of the tag, though Duke Ellington deserves it even more on the basis of his vast body of compositions and the nature of the "jungle style" music that first made him famous. Ellington's ten-man group of 1927–32 was billed for a time as the Jungle Band, a title in keeping with the Southern plantation/Afro-Deco interior and exotic-erotic floor shows of the Cotton Club, the grandest Harlem venue (it seated more than six hundred guests), where Ellington performed, before whites only, for five years, 1927–31, and the spring seasons of 1933, 1937, and 1938.

The fact of racial segregation is *musically* important since it focuses on putative Caucasian needs and expectations, the *frissons* and curative powers sought in "jungle" music and dance—the magic Josephine Baker had transported to Paris. A two-part 1929 record, "A Night at the Cotton Club," simulates a club performance, replete with applause and an overbearing announcer who salutes Ellington for creating "a real Hades in Harlem." Although Ellington recorded simultaneously for several companies, using different pseudonyms, the phrases "Jungle Band" and "jungle style" have rightly survived as generic labels for all the records that established Ellington's reputation, starting with such memorable early pieces as "Black and Tan Fantasy," "East St. Louis Toodle-oo," "Creole Love Call," "Jubilee Stomp," "The Mooche," and "Hot and Bothered," all from 1927–28, before Ellington was thirty.

OPPOSITE: 99. Alexander Calder, *Josephine Baker,* 1927–29. Wire. 39″ high. In the late twenties and thirties, Calder invariably carried coils of soft wire and pliers to social gatherings so he could "sketch" on the spot, in space. Wire coat hangers would suffice in a Jo Jones pinch.

The Jungle Band's most extraordinary sounds were produced by trumpeters Bubber Miley and Cootie Williams (who took Miley's place in 1929) and trombonist Joe Nanton, whose nickname "Tricky Sam" projected the essence of "jungle" techniques. Following the example of King Oliver, they developed a wider variety of often speechlike growling and *wa-wa* sounds by humming and/or gargling gutturally in their throats while blowing legitimate musical notes on brass instruments that were distorted by various metal mutes and/or the manual manipulation in front of the horn of a simple rubber toilet plunger ("the plumber's helper") deprived of its long wooden handle—the now-famous plunger mute. It was wielded most wondrously by Joe Nanton, whose sound effects, according to cornetist Rex Stewart, ranged "from the wail of a newborn baby to the raucous hoot of an owl, from the bloodcurdling scream of an enraged tiger to the eerie cooing of a mourning dove. Tricky had them all in his bag of tricks, and he utilized them with thoughtful discretion and good taste," says Stewart.

"Thoughtful" is the operative word, since the jungle style has long been mischaracterized as "primitive," which misses the boat, Congo River and Mississippi, too. Ellington's jungle exists on no map. Although his jungle style has been linked with the talking drum signals of Africa, it is as calculated an artistic construct as the self-conscious modernist primitivism of Brancusi (figs. 30, 31, 32) and the Africanesque paintings of Picasso, Derain, and Matisse. None of these men obtained their art supplies, plumbing equipment, or "Eurocentric" brass instruments at the jungle trading post. The only strange gods they jointly serve is the West's persistent notion that the possibility of a better elemental, passional life is passing us by and may exist somewhere else—in art environments like Brancusi's *Newborn,* perhaps, but not in life (fig. 83). Thanks to its anachronistic "ancient" Art Deco configurations, Brancusi's salvaged and carved pedestal runs dramatically in opposite directions, back toward primal wood and woods, including the Garden of Eden, and ahead to a life-enhancing contemporary structure such as the Chrysler Building (1928–31)—the equipoise created, too, by an Ellington "jungle" orchestration.

Although the connotations of "Jungle Band" may be offensive to current political sensibilities, its first clear masterpiece, "Black and Tan Fantasy," can be interpreted as an inspiring racial statement (the best is the RCA Victor version, recorded October 6, 1927, as opposed to three other similar versions recorded on different labels in the same month). The "Tan" of the title refers to light complexions, long deemed a social

100. Self-conscious primitivism for the record: jungle nights and the genteel fox-trot contained by rigorous, formal design, 1930.

advantage to African-Americans, starting with candidates for the chorus line at the Cotton Club, where color-consciousness informed more than one of the sketches that Ellington's band accompanied. However egregious or trite their content, these Cotton Club routines did stimulate and force Ellington and the Club's resident songwriter-arranger, Harold Arlen, to compose constantly, just as the most banal or uncertain carnival and vaudeville and nightclub acts challenged the imagination of Jo Jones, who told this writer that he once had to cover up the flatulence of a talking horse with "the loudest drum roll in history."

In one Cotton Club sketch circa 1929, a light-skinned, very muscular Negro aviator, wearing only shorts, headgear, and goggles, parachutes into the jungle of darkest Africa to rescue a blond debutante white goddess from a band of tar-black painted savages. (There are few accounts of Cotton Club sketches and no documentation of which recorded Ellington numbers might have accompanied them, though such titles as "Hottentot," "Jungle Stomp," and "Jungle Nights in Harlem" sound all-purpose.) The dirge tempo of "Black and Tan Fantasy" would have disqualified it as background music for the rescue sketch, but it surely addresses its racial issues. Co-composed by Bubber Miley and Ellington, it comprises two minor and major blues choruses. Miley's mournful second plunger solo, following Nanton's, concludes by unexpectedly quoting Chopin's *Funeral March,* a readily identifiable allusion. (The solos may well have been composed to begin with, or written out after an initial improvisation, since all subsequent recordings and performances stick very close to the original recording.) A funeral march is appropriate if Ellington is grieving that the race issue—crippling color-consciousness and self-hatred among blacks, simple bigotry almost everywhere else—could prove the death of America. "The Black and Tan," Ellington told Stanley Dance in 1962, "was a speakeasy of the period where people of all races and colors mixed together." Ellington's fantasy proposes music as a healing, multicultural balm, comic relief included. Tricky Sam Nanton's trombone horse-whinny at the end of his plaintive plunger solo points to the nag pulling the coffin and the *fun* in "funeral," to try to replicate the wit and ebullience that's invariably around the bend in Duke's jungle.

The union of the blues and Chopin is a great moment, Miley leading the ensemble from one musical strain into another as seamlessly as Brancusi carving each subsequent serration on his *King of Kings* or Ellington swinging Tchaikovsky's *Nutcracker Suite* in 1960 (partly orchestrated by Strayhorn), the culminating marvel and joy of jazz multiculturalism. The latter is expressed with patriotic fervor in an extended, five-minute version of "St. Louis Blues" recorded "live" on the evening of November 7, 1940, at a dance at the Crystal Ballroom in Fargo, North Dakota. It's the closing number, rousing but rough, as though they had no formal arrangement; this band never did record it commercially. (Ellington recorded it in 1928.) The tempo is uncommonly fast for this song, and Ellington lets his soloists loose. It ends on a multicultural chord with the band quoting the main theme from "Black and Tan Fantasy" followed quickly by the famous *Rhapsody in Blue* fanfare that Armstrong quoted in every performance of Waller's "Black and Blue." After several more moments, which include Ellington's spoken "Good night and thank you," the orchestra launches into an eighteen-second version (it fades away) of Irving Berlin's "God Bless America"—generated spontaneously, it seems, because they sound like a high-school marching band at its first rehearsal. Ellington had never before performed "God Bless America" (famously recorded by Kate Smith in 1939), and would never repeat this airing. Why did he offer it at Fargo?

If you accept Ellington's truncated "God Bless America" as a delayed coda or postscript to "St. Louis Blues," it introduces the idea of producing multicultural medleys for regions in need, such as North Dakota, a seriously Caucasian state. On the political level, Franklin D. Roosevelt, much loved by Negro voters, had been reelected the day before, November 6, for an unprecedented third term, and the current issue of *LIFE* was celebrating the American electoral ideal with a cover photo of a smiling crowd of flag-waving citizens, captioned DEMOCRACY: 50 MILLION VOTERS (November 4, 1940). Wouldn't you have played "God Bless America," the unofficial second national anthem (written by an immigrant, Irving Berlin), if you had a band at your command and believed in the full democratic potential of our land? A poem, forsooth!—to complement the good cheer at the Crystal Ballroom on November 7, 1940, exemplified by Tricky Sam Nanton, who begins his solo on "St. Louis Blues" by bleating three *wa-wa* bars of "Whistle While You Work," the dwarfs' song in *Snow White* (1938)—no loose St. Louis woman, she—followed by a blatant blues cliché as parody clears the way for the trombonist's six choruses of inspired self-expression along a fresh jungle path, the entire ensemble riffing very loud moans and groans behind Nanton as they rush toward their concluding "Black and Tan"/Gershwin conflation. It is stated out-of-tempo, raucously, a bus screeching to a stop. What did the dancers in

Fargo make of the jungle style and mix of allusions? Musicians, especially colored ones, could seem mysterious. "When any group, any performers, come to town, don't people always come out and hover near, leaning inward about them, to learn what it is? What is it? Listen," writes Eudora Welty early in "Powerhouse." "Watch them carefully, hear the least word, especially what they say to one another, in another language. . . ."

"God Bless America" proclaimed by African-Americans straightforwardly, without irony, bespeaks the bracing equanimity shared by Armstrong, Waller, and Ellington, no small moral achievement, especially in view of flaws in the jazznocracy such as the way black swing bands lost bookings to inferior white bands owing to racial restrictions. (Certain "white" hotels in New York City wouldn't hire Ellington, Basie, or Ella Fitzgerald until the late 1940s.) Ellington's 1962 tribute to twenty-four big bands, white and black, of the 1925–55 period, is thus magnanimous on several levels, especially his respectful treatment of popular but corny and jazz-free white dance bands such as those led by Ben Bernie, Fred Waring (with Glee Club!), Wayne King, and Guy Lombardo—all dimly remembered now, but Ellington's colleagues then, equally determined to serve the needs and expectations of dancers, not jazz critics. (The attendance record at Harlem's Savoy Ballroom was set by Lombardo.) Ellington's new arrangements of either the theme songs or the most representative numbers of the big bands are tantamount to a massive Armstrong/Waller rescue operation because the listener's respect and/or nostalgic affection for these familiar songs—e.g., Tommy Dorsey's "I'm Gettin' Sentimental Over You"— would seem to rule out any tampering. But Ellington's old collage try succeeds wondrously. Most notable are his versions of Stan Kenton's "Artistry in Rhythm" (the work of eight brass drolly transferred to the solo violin of Ray Nance) and Lombardo's "Auld Lang Syne," a masterpiece of creative recycling on a par with the *Nutcracker* and *Peer Gynt Suite* orchestrations. Ellington meets this challenge head-on by improving upon Lombardo's basic appeal: sweet melody played meticulously by his saxophones. Ellington's pliable saxophone section delivers "Auld Lang Syne" in a luxurious manner—a *Normandie* or *Queen Mary* glide, ballast provided by the broad and deep sound of Harry Carney's baritone saxophone, discrete punctuation by *doo-wah doo-wah* figures from the well-mannered brass players. Matisse's *The Swimmer in the Pool* records this saxophone glide, basic black suiting the fact that it's New Year's Eve (fig. 101). Cootie Williams, back with Ellington after a twelve-year absence, takes a short, jungle style plunger solo that adds some amusing, anachronistic multicultural grit to the traditional Scottish ditty and its tuxedo junction.

The "Auld Lang Syne" title alone functions like an ideal literary/cultural allusion, novelistic shorthand that returns old readers to the New Year's Eves of yore, when TV viewers at home vicariously participated in Lombardo's annual celebrations (1947–77) of optimism at New York's jam-packed Hotel Roosevelt, whose name connects bands of every stripe with the idea of serving the social good. If people were waiting at a ballroom somewhere in North Dakota or Mississippi, the band bus had to get through the rain or snow despite any poor roads. "God Bless American Big Bands," Ellington's generous 1962 tributes state in effect. God would in fact be invoked most grandiloquently by Ellington in the 1960s, *his* sixties.

Allusions in Ellington ranging from Chopin to Disney parallel the "intertextual" modernist manner of Eliot, Joyce, and Pound, which helps to define "Black and Tan Fantasy" as the first work of black modernism, however academic the designation. Of course its rank isn't as apparent as the position of Gertrude Stein's *Three Lives* (1909) as the historical cornerstone of American experimental prose modernism, even if the book's life now depends solely on university and college syllabi and the pass Stein gets for her persistent primitivist racialism. ("Rose had the simple, promiscuous unmorality of the black people," Stein typically writes in "Melanctha.") The racial reading of "Black and Tan Fantasy" and gloss on "St. Louis Blues" are of course blatantly "literary," which doesn't go against the grain of Ellington. His career-long involvement with language is more interesting than he himself would have realized, starting with his stage patter and persona, which was variously charming, ingratiating, and unctuous, the latter in a myriad of fulsome, slyly insincere, constantly shifting shades—a put-on, expressing . . . who knows? "Mask is the key word," as Humbert says. Ellington seems to be wearing lipstick in the caricature that adorned the music stands of his players in 1942–43—a good metaphor or metonym for his range of artifice (fig. 102). Analysis, however "literary," must distinguish the trees from the jungle.

The speechlike intonations of the jungle style are related to Armstrong's scat but more radical because the jungle style doesn't begin

OVERLEAF: 101. Henri Matisse, *The Swimmer in the Pool,* from *Jazz,* 1947.

102. Artist unknown, caricature of Duke Ellington that adorned music stands of the Orchestra, 1942–43, and the cover of the 1942 RCA Victor album *A Duke Ellington Panorama,* the first reissue of his early masterpieces.

with comprehensible language. (Armstrong eschewed the plunger, despite its importance to his mentor, King Oliver, in favor of scat.) Where the lyrics of certain Armstrong numbers allow that his secret language of scat addresses sex and race, the brass growls of Nanton and Miley and wordless scat singing of Baby Cox on "Hot and Bothered" and "The Mooche" (the recording of October 1, 1928) are nondiscursive and teasing. As usual, Tricky Sam sounds as though he's really trying to talk, but all efforts to discern meaning are as frustrating and funny as attempts to comprehend the needs of our barking dog or earnestly babbling eighteen-month-old baby. It's not only a joke, though, if Ellington is trying to distill and communicate his sense of the African-American experience, which is hardly a presumptuous surmise, given the titles of Ellington's subsequent, extended works: *Black, Brown, and Beige* (1943–46); *A Tone Parallel to Harlem (The Harlem Suite)* (1951); and *My People* (1963). In 1928, the composer of "The Mooche" could have explained, "words fail"—we know the failure—and added, "That's why we have music." The titles of many songs from his great 1940–42 period are "musical" in that they alone traverse a happy tumult without being precise: "Cottontail"; "Conga Brava"; "Bli-Blip"; "Jumpin' Punkins"; "Hayfoot Strawfoot"—poetic feets, whatever they mean. The title of Ellington's 1928 "The Blues with a Feelin' " is purposefully open-ended. Full emphasis should fall on the vague final word—no proper or improper nouns are provided, no St. Louis or empty-bed blues are cited, no hint of any "Brava." Fill in the blank with *your* feelings. Find the word(s). It's a challenge. On "Creole Love Song" (1932, from the experimental long-playing stereo version), Cootie Williams tries to keep a stiff upper lip, to growl rather than whine. His plaintive *wa-wa* solo almost articulates "Why? Why? Why? Why?" but not quite, preserving the sense of privacy if not dignity a singer would sacrifice in the process of overt expression, the risk taken by trumpeter Louis Bacon on "Dear Old Southland" (1933), a non-Ellington song based on "Deep River." Louis Bacon three times tries to sing "I wanna be—" only to stop short each time and groan "oh-uh-ohh," unable to complete the (futile dream?) lyric. "I wanna be—loved?" "—feel safe?" "—secure?" "—rich?" "—happy?" Johnny Hodges follows with a beautiful, lyrical soprano saxophone solo that suggests that at least four of those five wishes are within reach. "My man, Lily Pons," Charlie Parker once called Hodges.

The connotations of the spiritual-inspired "Dear Old Southland," Bacon's three words and groans, and Cootie's muffled "Why?" speak

African-American volumes—the ones that Toni Morrison, among others, is striving to write. But the shortcomings of Ellington's verbal narratives for *My People* and the *Second Sacred Concert* (1968) demonstrate that his 1928 instincts were sounder and that bigger is not necessarily better. The toilet plunger, as vernacular and democratic as an object gets, is the source of the most popular incarnation of avant-garde aleatory music. This is a major Ellington achievement, totally unremarked by the musicologists and critics who would readily admit that—save for movie soundtracks—aleatory music, from Pierre Boulez down, has not found an audience. Ellington's jungle style is Varèse for the people by way of the plumber.

This may sound like qualified praise indeed, inasmuch as Ellington's stature is now a sensitive, charged issue. Serious discussion of Ellington is vexed by the promotion of him as the greatest American or twentieth-century composer, classical music included. It is therefore good to remember, in this prestige-conscious and very politicized time, that Ellington's reputation was enhanced as early as 1927 by highbrow praise of his miniatures alone, recordings that are, at most, three minutes and thirty seconds long. (Mark Tucker has collected the early appraisals in his excellent 1993 book, *The Duke Ellington Reader.*) Ellington's reputation does not depend on his extended compositions. The latter do not have to be deemed better than, say, Aaron Copland's for Ellington to remain "beyond category," to use the highest praise Ellington himself could bestow. Ellington's phrase should allow us to step fairly around the problematic tag "greatest," as Charlie Parker did: "It's all music, man."

In 1932, Ellington expanded his band to fourteen musicians and, with less call for Cotton Club scores, began to enlarge his orchestral palette well beyond the jungle style, a broadening that's been misunderstood. Even Joe Nanton was allowed to voice human truths without imitating animals. On "Dear Old Southland," for instance, he plays too loudly and busily over rather than behind Louis Bacon's attempts to sing, but it's purposeful. The listener almost misses the fact that Bacon is near tears. For a change, Nanton is imitating a very kind person who's coughing to cover up a friend's gaucherie—a growth in dramatic range equivalent to the ambitions and advances of Duke Ellington and His Famous Orchestra, as it was now billed. Ravel, it was said, had influenced the new Ellington, whose "Solitude" (1934) might be called Afro-French Impressionism thanks to its mellifluous saxophone scoring, its subdued brass passages, and Artie Whetsol's lovely, astonishingly quiet open trumpet solo—low volume without any loss of tone. In 1934 the English composer and critic Constant Lambert wrote of 1928's "Hot and Bothered": "I know of nothing in Ravel so dextrous in treatment as the varied solos in the middle . . . and nothing in Stravinsky more dynamic than the final section." Gunther Schuller, an Ellington admirer, thinks this is extravagant and doubts that Ellington had even heard Ravel at this point. But highbrow praise such as Lambert's and Percy Grainger's (he ranked Ellington with Bach and Delius) set the tone and trajectory of subsequent commentary on Ellington, which has usually asserted or implied that the composer eschewed the jungle style after 1934 as he progressed toward his prime achievement, the 1940–42 orchestra. This is wrong, and worth arguing if it deepens an appreciation of that band's subtlety and range.

Simply stated, as Ellington's post–Cotton Club arrangements evolved in the thirties, the jungle idea—vamps, blue interludes, growls—receded from the conceptual center, making room for as many as five soloists on a piece, only one or two of them in the jungle manner (Nanton, Williams, Stewart), and not necessarily on every number. Sudden bursts of self-conscious primitivism now helped to create a range of startling contrasts in the more complex and densely textured orchestrations of 1940–42, especially since they are cushioned by the richer sound banks achieved by the saxophone section, expanded to five with the addition of Ben Webster's tenor in late 1939. By turns volcanic and lyrical ("Rosebud," he seems about to whisper at the end of ballads), Webster became the band's most compelling solo voice, a jungle player without plunger whose tone, on up-tempo numbers, sometimes took on the angry rasp of hornets and wasps on the loose.

Judicious jungle style solos add bite to many of the most civilized arrangements for the 1940–42 orchestra (the recordings mentioned here are by this edition of the band). "Ko-Ko," from the first recording session of the 1940–42 orchestra and one of its greatest works (no relation to Charlie Parker's "Koko"), opens with an aggressive, almost defiant plunger solo by Tricky Sam Nanton, as if to say, "Musical advances aren't going to make *me* take a back seat in your train or trolley," as he soon demonstrated in Fargo with his "St. Louis Blues" solo. "Ko-Ko" is in fact based on only a twelve-bar minor blues, Ellington challenging himself to make the most of the least, like limited-vocabulary Hemingway or Stuart Davis, who needs only one word from the jazz lexicon, "Pad," to stress *Standard Brand*'s dancing, rising pulse (fig. 15). Ellington never loses touch with the vernacular, either, opening many of his "advanced" arrangements almost alone at the piano, as in "Across the Track Blues," accompanied only by his brilliant young bassist Jimmie Blanton and drummer Sonny Greer on brushes, and then Barney Bigard may enter gently on clarinet. They vamp together momentarily, Duke playing sparely, daydreaming at the piano, it seems, coming up with the next number quickly beneath an empty mural space that will shortly accommodate a busy crew of sophisticated colorists and the plumber's helpers, too, a noisy union.

Plungers musically fix everyday moments we all know. On "The Giddybug Gallop," a very up-tempo train number, Sonny Greer swooshes his brushes (not sticks) heavily to simulate the wheels of a crowded train pulling out of the station so fast that Tricky Sam Nanton, on his feet in the unsteady car, is jostled this way and that so rudely that he solos immediately, sputtering and complaining loudly like an ordinary guy but through a plunger mute: Why don't somebody give a poor ol' trombonist a hand or seat? In "John Hardy's Wife," the characteristically smooth ensemble performance is suddenly interrupted by the agitated, antic, plunger-driven, and half-valve squawking of cornetist Rex Stewart as Hardy's henpecking wife (the title in fact draws on the band's own name for a threatening gal), whom Lawrence Brown, nicknamed the Deacon for his proper bearing, answers with a mollifying, creamy-toned trombone solo, the soothing five-man saxophone section rolling in as one to apply more salve—an accurate projection, as it happens, of Ellington's well-known compulsion to avoid all personal unpleasantness. "In a Mellowtone," based on the chords of "Rose Room," is highlighted by a sequence of sixteen swift two- and four-bar conversational exchanges between the muted, querulous trumpet of Cootie Williams and the unison, swelling lines of the ever-so-soigné saxophone section—Dionysus versus Apollo, or the id, ego, and superego figuring out how to keep everything mellow.

Jungle effects, especially Nanton's, are crucial in rescue operations of non-Ellington stuff, growing funnier, it seems, with every advance of the Ducal reputation. "Chloe (Song of the Swamp)," a foolish 1927 number that had been sung to death, opens with Tricky Sam whining the melody through his plunger mute, which sounds more like *yoi-yoi* than *wa-wa,* a Yiddish complaint in the jungle that should make us grin and sets us up for surprising delights when we're treated to a series of beautiful statements rather than further eccentric turns—silken scoring for the five saxophones (by Ellington's assistant, Billy Strayhorn); a dulcet, dignified bit by trombonist Lawrence Brown; and the wistfulness of Ben Webster's measured solo—all played off Nanton's antic, jagged-edged opening. In "The Sidewalks of New York," four gallant soloists improvise uphill on the 1904 chestnut only to have Tricky Sam assume the unexpected role of straight man at the end and anticlimactically play the familiar melody so faithfully through his muted plunger that it's impossible not to remember the lyrics and laugh: "East Side, West Side / All around the town." Where is that jungle message coming from? Central Park? On "The 'C' Jam Blues," Nanton's speechlike plunger growling almost forms a comprehensible phonetic statement that urges his leader to "keep the game preserve open," which Ellington did, having recently recorded the comically outrageous and gamy "Menelik (The Lion of Judah)" and the tender "A Portrait of Bert Williams." The latter pays tribute to the much-loved but now forgotten Negro blackface comedian. Barney Bigard's gentle, tentative clarinet solo is said to emulate Williams's halting speech, but Nanton concludes with a stabbing, oblique plunger solo whose plaintive hints of speech only point to the mystery of Williams's complex persona and Ellington's 1928 philosophy of language.

Although mutes and plungers most often serve comic purposes in arrangements from 1940–42, Ellington's use of them in the trumpet showcases of the time makes more direct human sense than ever before, as in "Concerto for Cootie," who opens his solo by playing quaveringly with a plunger over an already cup-muted trumpet bell, grandly removing these fetters on his magisterial second chorus to release Armstrong-like open joys. But after only half a chorus, he tamps and conserves them with another, even tighter mute, evidently to meet tomorrow's anticipated needs. They seem to ride on "Take the 'A' Train" (composed by Strayhorn), where Williams's replacement in the band, Ray Nance, removes *his* mute unconditionally after two sonically subdued choruses and quickly ascends the subway stairs to a brilliant, open-horned Harlem day on 125th Street, no doubt, since it was the main stop and main stem, to use the wonderfully organic jive idiom for the most-happenin' avenue in every town and city. Ellington's "Main Stem," a twelve-bar blues that isn't blue, celebrates their collective vitality by letting seven men solo (the most ever), including Deacon Lawrence Brown, for once as rambunctious as Nanton, whose raunchy plunger statement affirms the stem. The plunger is just as hortatory a device to Ray Nance, who opens *The Harlem Suite* (1951) with a two-note plunger articulation: "Har-lem," a telescopic Ellington moment. The plunger and its sound potential clearly represent and render the deepest, most ineffable reaches of the composer's racial consciousness.

A wickedly ironic aspect of Ellington's musical wit was his deployment of the jungle style against both racial stereotyping and false racial consciousness or pride. Cootie Williams takes down "Ol' Man River" (1938) as the nominal leader of a small Ellington unit called Cootie Williams and His Rug Cutters. (Stellar sidemen such as Williams, Rex Stewart, Johnny Hodges, and Barney Bigard made some one hundred recordings between 1936 and 1941 under their own names, though the piano player—Ellington or Strayhorn—invariably called the shots.) Although "Ol' Man River" had gained national operatic status as sung by Paul Robeson (not yet a racial hero) in the 1936 film version of *Show Boat* (1927), Ellington and Williams treat the Jerome Kern–Oscar Hammerstein aria as a pretentious darky number. They render "Ol' Man River" absurd by assigning the vocal to a mediocre female singer, Jerry Kruger. "You and me, we sweat and strain," she pipes sweetly, and we have to smile, no less than if a bear-chested Fats Waller were singing in falsetto. She takes liberties with the lyrics, primly refining its Black English and interpolating a new line: "Smoke a little tea [marijuana] / And sing *o sole mee-uh.*" But Cootie Williams follows the letter, his plunger solo phonetically rendering the familiar opening lines with syllabic exactitude; if one knows the melody, the considerable humor even comes across on the page. "Ol' man river, dat ol' man river" (plus other lines) are growled as *"wa-wa wa-wa, wa wa-wa-WAH-wa,"* and so forth. "Ol' Man River," always sung rubato, is taken up-tempo against all prevailing currents by Cootie and the Rug Cutters, which makes us visualize the stevedores, male and female (shirts optional), liftin' an' totin' at a comically impossible pace, rushing back and forth, herky-jerky, as in a speeded-up old slapstick comedy—Mack Sennett in blackface, *Show Boat* aground. Satire and brass can bring down any construct, especially if it's as combustible as the idea of minstrelsy. The denizens of Walker Evans' 1936 minstrel show poster seem self-reflexively amazed by their own demise and the fact that the attack pack is Negro—in reality, Armstrong, Waller, and Ellington and his "Trumpet No End" (the title of a 1946 number, the trumpet section expanded to an explosive five).

The Rug Cutters' attack on "Ol' Man River" is seriously and acceptably "phallocentric" in its comic reclaiming of African-American manhood. Given Ellington's status, however, not even the highest note screeching of his long-time trumpeter Cat Anderson was ever termed tasteless or "phallocentric," just as Calder's childlike aura has kept

103. Alexander Calder, *Obus,* 1972. Sheet metal, bolts, and paint. 12′ high.

critics from identifying his huge outdoor stabile *Obus* (1972) as another incarnation of antiquity's phallic altar of Dionysus (see Picasso's,
fig. 80), now enviably fortified against the cold and old age by "red
weather" vessels and airy sheet-metal testicles designed to accommodate the wind (fig. 103).

   "Ol' Man River" has been denuded completely by the Ellingtonians, akin to the way Calder's wire sculpture *Josephine Baker* (1927–29)
reduces Colin's caricature (fig. 19), Baker's new liplessness marking
radical progress (fig. 99). The mandalas are operative, Calder's soul
through Baker's ample body; in art gallery profile, her fore and aft stick
way out, no one's notion of wiry. The Rug Cutters' "Ol' Man River" is
on the level of "That's Why Darkies Were Born," as sung by Frank
Munn, who in fact had a leading role in the 1932 Broadway revival of
Show Boat. The bass-baritone Noble Negro is now just another black
buck in an ignoble revue. "Give him a parachute," Ellington could be
saying, as though commenting on the Cotton Club's wretched jungle
rescue sketch. "Buckle it up tight. Now jump!" commands Duke, cast-
ing aside the masks, letting loose like Powerhouse. *Jump for Joy,* Ellington's stage musical of 1941, presented in Los Angeles, was a witty
frontal attack on racial injustice and stereotypes (book and lyrics by
Paul Francis Webster and Sid Kuller), a demolition of Josephine
Baker's jungle prison (fig. 19). Backed by the full Ellington Orchestra,
Herb Jeffries sings the show's title tune with a stentorian tone worthy
of a spiritual: "Fare thee well, land of cotton / Cotton lille [lace] is out
of style / Honey chile—jump for joy! / Don't you grieve little Eve [from
Uncle Tom's Cabin] / All the hounds I do believe / Have been killed /
Ain't you thrilled? Jump for joy!" "Oh, *Green Pastures* was just a Tech-
nicolor movie," Jeffries sings, dismissing the 1936 film version of Connelly's *Green Pastures,* historically important as the most respected
racially condescending production of its time and a standard inclusion
in *Great American Plays* anthologies into the 1950s. Its dismissal here is
a radical act. "In *Jump for Joy,* Uncle Tom is dead. God rest his bones,"

OPPOSITE: 104. Although *Cabin in the Sky* (1943) is said to be the least condescending of "race" films, this clever poster offers prospective bigoted white viewers familiar, inviting stereotypes at the same time that it posits for Negroes a
compelling "Black and Tan Fantasy": the woman's upper body is pitch black but
her leg is ambiguously pale. Is an African-American turning white before our
eyes? Or is she wearing an orthopedic stocking?

105. Walker Evans, *Minstrel Showbill Detail,* Alabama, 1936.

106. Cootie Williams, 1947. Photograph by Popsie Randolph.

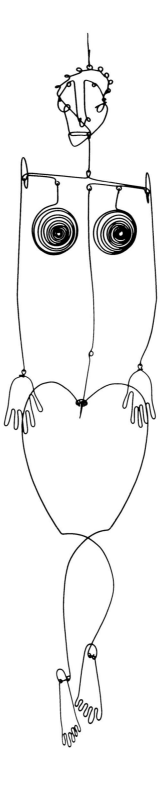

107. Alexander Calder, *Aztec Josephine Baker*, 1930. Wire. 4.5′ high.

wrote an ecstatic reviewer in the *Los Angeles Tribune,* a Negro weekly newspaper. Fittingly, the title tune opens with Tricky Sam Nanton growling the as-yet-unheard lyrics with phonetic literalness, a respectful prefiguration and droll stomp of approval on the demise of the cotton locus and culture. Webster and Hodges solo emphatically and the ensemble does jump for joy, having made its unambiguous main statement in plain English, so crucial to Armstrong, Waller, and Joyce, in more than one chapter of *Ulysses.*

The Cotton Club had recently closed its doors forever, but it would be disingenuous to call this significant since Uncle Tom was hardly dead and gone. Walker Evans' eviscerated, disappearing plantation-mammy (lower right, fig. 105) seems to be clearing the way for Faulkner's stalwart Dilsey in *The Sound and the Fury* (1929) and the cheerily bossy Beulah of 1940s radio (Hattie McDaniel, atoning for the handkerchief-head she'd played in *Gone With the Wind*). In truth, however, Evans' showbill mammy was still intact in the Aunt Jemima pancake ads that continued to appear regularly in *LIFE.* "Here 'tis! My temptilatin' Old-Time Buckwheat Menu!" she declares in a speech-balloon (January 20, 1941). It's enough to take the spring out of one of Calder's wired Josephine Bakers.

Even more noteworthy than the "Jump for Joy" statement is another 1941 Ellington occasion, the recording of "Menelik (The Lion of Judah)," by an eight-man Ellington group led by Rex Stewart, the Calder of the cornet, whose uninhibited behavior as man and musician had earned him the nickname "Boy." ("Boy Meets Horn" [1938], with its witty half-valving, was Stewart's most famous solo feature with Ellington.) "Menelik (The Lion of Judah)" is said to be a tribute to Haile Selassie, the emperor of Ethiopia (1930–74) and titular Lion. He had become an international cultural hero to blacks and whites alike in 1936 after Mussolini's modern army had easily overwhelmed and conquered Ethiopia's spear-bearing defenders, and Selassie's personal plea before the assembled League of Nations had fallen on unsympathetic ears. He fled to British protection and, in 1941, following Italian defeats, regained his throne with British support, much to the delight of everyone—except Ellington, it seems.

Stewart opens "Menelik" (one of Selassie's royal family names) over rolling tom-toms with his plunger-mute version of a lion's roar, a low-comedy, tone-free, growling, rumbling alimentary sound in very dubious taste, signaling acute indigestion at the Central Park Zoo. This surprisingly irreverent beginning, extending Waller's range of sound effects, is followed by some stately enough open-horn tooting topped by Stewart's closing "roar," where good taste is thrown to the winds, truly, and his bottom notes sound like dangerous flatulence. No child of any age could fail to recognize and laugh at the first-grade fun wrought by bad boy Rex, King of the Jungle Style, on this day, anyway. The plumber's helper, handle intact, is more than apt as scepter and emergency measure. The Lion has fallen, much like "Ol' Man River," "Old Plantation" (Waller), and "Shine."

Rex, with Ellington's backing, *is* kingly, asserting his independence bravely, in the face of Selassie's undeserved status. The mock tribute speaks to current pretensions and follies in the areas of Afrocentrism, identity politics, and the false gods of sports and entertainment. Selassie was in truth a petty despot indifferent to the poverty of his subjects, a colonial pawn, a toothless lion who maintained his grandiose claim to be the 111th descendent of King Solomon and the Queen of Sheba—roots to spare, and rib. Small wonder the executives at RCA Victor rejected the record, finding it in poor taste, one guesses, or unacceptably disrespectful to the Lion of Judah, or too reminiscent of the sometimes alimentary musical burlesque performed by Spike Jones and His City Slickers. "Menelik" went unreleased in this country until circa 1953, when it appeared on a Rex Stewart LP. It qualifies as the band's most outrageous jungle music since the title figure in "Arabian Lover" (1929) turned out to be a camel in heat, or so Nanton's plunger-work suggests, in a number that definitively mocks that area of exotica—Rudolph Valentino, cinema's "Arabian lover" in *The Sheik* (1921) and *Son of the Sheik* (1926)—drummer Sonny Greer replicating hot hoofbeats, somehow. Adepts of aleatory music might ask, How did Greer do this? Coconut shells on blocks of wood? Doesn't that alone sound like a museum-bound neo-Dadaist work possibly titled *Sheik Dumb*? And professors pursuing postcolonial studies could reasonably term Ellington's "Arabian Lover" a serious critique of orientalism before the letter—to grab at any (camel) straw to get Ellington into the current curriculum.

The musical flatulence of "Menelik" might have been accepted by the more enlightened executives at RCA if someone had thought to place it in line with the experiments of Varèse and the Joyce who created "Sirens," the elaborately wrought "aleatory" chapter of *Ulysses*. Joyce is of course the most musical of prose-poets, and writes to please the ear more than the eye. "Clapclop. Clipclap. Clappyclap," Joyce writes on the first page of "Sirens" (*Ulysses,* page 256), which sustains the contrapuntal play of verbal themes, songs, and sounds ranging from hoofbeats and the expanding tap-tapping of a blind man's cane to the accelerated rumblings of Mr. Bloom's upper and lower digestive tracks. The delicately orchestrated aleatory prose of the chapter's five last pages incorporates the onomatopoetic libretto that Rex Stewart could have been following in "Menelik": "Rrr" at first (page 287), then "Rrrrr" (289), and then "Prrprr" and "Fff. Oo. Rrpr" on the last page, concluded in its closing lines by "Karaaaaaaa" and "Pprrpffrrppffff" (291). Bloom's explosive fart (to drain it of its music and poetry) is counterpointed by Mr. Bloom's fragmented italicized phrases recollected from the once-famous courtroom speech of the doomed Irish patriot, Robert Emmet, Bloom counting off like Rex Stewart or a rocketeer: "One. Two. *Let my epitaph be.* Karaaaaaaaa." Joyce's political point about gaseous rhetoric and false consciousness is analogous to Stewart's lionizing of Haile Selassie.

No doubt most readers miss Joyce's political tack, but it does set up the very next chapter, "Cyclops," whose parodies of gassy patriotism, racial chauvinism, absurd snobbery, and cheap journalism are comprehensible, unlike the "Oxen of the Sun," because Joyce's mass-culture targets in "Cyclops" are recognizable in their present incarnations. The despair and sense of failure that fuels Afrocentrism and other manifestations of compensatory self-celebration are comically captured by Joyce's wild vision of a massive primordial kilted Celt from whose "girdle hung a row of seastones which dangled at every movement of his portentous frame and on these were graven with rude yet striking art the tribal images of many Irish heroes and heroines of antiquity . . . [including] . . . Captain Moonlight, Captain Boycott, Dante Alighieri, Christopher Columbus, S. Fursa, S. Brendan, Marshal MacMahon, Charlemagne, Theobald Wolfe Tone, the Mother of the Maccabees, the Last of the Mohicans, the Rose of Castile, the Man for Galway, the Man that Broke the Bank at Monte Carlo, the Man in the Gap, the Woman Who Didn't, Benjamin Franklin, Napoleon Bonaparte, John L. Sullivan, Cleopatra, Savoureen Deelish, Julius Caesar, Paracelsus, Sir Thomas Lipton, William Tell, Michelangelo, Hayes," and seventy-five more Irish heroes and heroines, six or seven of whom are actually Irish, Hayes included. *Hayes?* Who is Hayes? Evidently Irish heroes are in short supply, and first names aren't required (page 297). Unexpected delight, out of the blue—that's what we expect of classic jazz. Joyce's brimming comic catalogs of names seem to gain force and velocity as they rush on and risk a traffic jam and chaos, like Ellington's five trum-

108. Artist unknown, 1940.

109. Friedrich Seidenstücker, *House Painters,* 1928, Germany.

peters trading lightning choruses in "Trumpet No End" (based on Irving Berlin's "Blue Skies") or a twenties photographer such as Friedrich Seidenstücker (fig. 109) flying through space shooting the street below from the point of view of Superman or Captain Marvel (fig. 108). Felicity must be around the bend.

Mr. Bloom assumes the mantle of Superjew in "Circe," the grand vaudevillian two-hundred-page chapter and focal point whose often outrageous midnight stage-play imaginings—authorial hallucinations in the main—reveal the truth about the diurnal events and psychological mental sets of even the most minor characters in *Ulysses*. Theodore Purefoy, whose wife gave birth in the previous chapter, here appears as a reluctant father and walking condom *"In fishing cap and oilskin jacket"* (note the italicized "stage" directions) who disparages by rote anyone who would employ "a mechanical device to frustrate the sacred ends of nature" (page 491). Although the irreligious Bloom is a Catholic convert and his mother was Protestant, Dublin only thinks of him as a Jew. He encounters anti-Semitism everywhere, and is even called "a coon" (page 106). The lyrics of "Black and Blue" could be adjusted easily to fit Mr. Bloom. In "Circe," however, compensatory fantasy thrives, as it did in Cleveland in the 1930s, when two shy, teenaged Jewish boys created Clark Kent/Superman. Mr. Bloom is declared Lord Mayor of Dublin (page 478) and quickly elevated to "undoubted emperor president and king chairman, the most serene and potent and very puissant ruler of this realm. God save Leopold the First!" the Bishop says of Bloom (page 482), who in turn shows everyone "that he is wearing green socks" (page 483). The ruler-designate is as insecure as a teenager switching schools; Joyce stages assimilation as a multicultural farce: *"A fife and drum band is heard in the distance playing the Kol Nidre"* (page 480). Bloom heralds the "new Bloomusalem," which, constructed immediately, features *"a collosal edifice, with crystal roof, built in the shape of a huge pork kidney, containing forty thousand rooms"* (page 484). The monumentalized pork-kidney architecture—anticipating an amusingly designed postmodern dialysis center—also conflates and celebrates ignoble appetites: the only meat proscribed by Jewish dietary laws and sensuous Mr. Bloom's delight in urinary odors and—we'll scat the rest or use the plunger.

The rams' horns sound and the standard of Zion is hoisted as Leopold the First is installed, unrolling a scroll and reading it aloud solemnly: "Aleph Beth Ghimel Daleth Hagadah Tephilim Kosher Yom Kippur Hanukah Roschaschana Beni Brith Bar Mitzvah Mazzoth

Askenazim Meshuggah Talith" (page 487). This nonsensical hodge-podge opens with the first four letters of the Hebrew alphabet, yokes three religious holidays, drops in a Jewish fraternal group ("Beni Brith"), prayer shawl ("Talith"), and the only Yiddish word Bloom uses elsewhere in *Ulysses* ("Meshuggah"). "Tephilim" (or *tefillin*), which few Christians could identify or explain—the little black leather boxes containing holy writ and worn on the head or arm by Orthodox Jews—is followed pointlessly by the commonplace "Kosher" because these constitute bits of a verbal salad or stew that renders the plight of Bloom, the deracinated Jew: "neither fish nor fowl" (page 3 2 1), rootless, utterly vulnerable.

An official translation of Bloom's nonlinear declaration is read aloud immediately by Jimmy Henry, assistant town clerk: "The Court of Conscience is now open. His Most Catholic Majesty will now administer open air justice. Free medical and legal advice, solution of doubles and other problems. All cordially invited . . ." Jimmy Henry automatically rejects Jewishness (not a joke) and reasserts the reigning culture's newly humane hegemony (the free advice). This outré comedy depends on the unambiguous meaning of Mr. Bloom's declaration, which is communicated by solid information and the reader's knowledge that the "Hebrew" doesn't add up—a refutation, today, of deconstruction's influential notion that the meaning of words is indeterminate. "Translator" Jimmy Henry obviously runs away with the theory.

His confidence boosted, the "new" Bloom conducts his antic Court of Conscience with *"rollicking humor."* "What is the parallax of the subsolar ecliptic of Aldebaran?" Chris Callinan asks His Highness. "Pleased to hear from you, Chris K. II," replies Bloom, exercising a charming and startling omniscience, since he's never seen this man before. (Joyce is showing his hand.) "This is indeed a festivity," says Crofton. "You call it a festivity. I call it a sacrament," states Bloom, who doesn't possess any instinctive sense of leadership or royal decorum. "Give us a tune, Bloom, one of the old sweet songs," urges Nosey Flynn, and Bloom obliges enthusiastically. "What railway opera is like a tramline in Gibraltar? The Rows of Casteele," Bloom answers himself, recycling an old gag in his effort to be accepted by the tense populace. "Plagiarist!" snorts Lenehan. "I'd give my life for [Bloom], the funniest man on earth," says the Veiled Sibyl. "I bet she's a bonny lassie," says Bloom, winking at the bystanders and indulging in Emerald Isle vernacular for the first time—the coon applying whiteface thickly. "Stage Irishman!" snarls Paddy Leonard, lacking any understanding or sympathy for the outsider-assimilationist with his anxious zeal (pages 488–91).

Needy Bloom's jerry-built "Judaism" is perceptive sociology, akin to the catalog of "Irish" heroes in "Cyclops" and a prefiguration of recent minority tacks such as the creation of Kwanzaa as an instant tradition and some African-American resistance to a white presence in the jazz canon—a Jimmy Henry reflex. Like most of "Circe," however, Bloom's Hebrew declaration and Celtic impersonation are also authorial riffs as outlined by Saul Steinberg (fig. 68)—just two of the numerous, ebullient, rapid-fire improvisations in a long night's work by a brilliant, manic stand-up comedian or the Marx Brothers, whose most prominent screenwriter, S. J. Perelman, claimed Joyce as his primary inspiration. Did you know, by the way, that Mel Brooks has just completed a Broadway-bound musical version of *Heart of Darkness,* where his dying Kurtz cries, "The hora, the hora!"? Did you know that Captain Marvel is Jewish (né Markowitz)? If you want to see how easy it is to make Roy Lichtenstein–like Pop art, add a comic-book speech balloon to Marvel's cover and have him say "TODAY I AM A MAN!" He could be a member of the Circumcised, a choral group in "Circe" that sings sacred Hebrew texts (page 544). The Kisses, "Circe" 's female doo-woppers before the fact, commemorate the first youthful lovemaking of the Blooms—"Icky licky micky sticky for Leo! . . . Yummyumm Womwom!" (page 475)—and could be backup singers for Bette Midler. The Kisses' name sounds as up-to-date as the Circumcised, a new Jewish rock-'n'-roll band from Dublin. Who says that jazz modernism is dead?

Because Joyce possessed the largest proverbial antennae in Europe, Picasso's Apollinaire in truth, he may have heard the first jazz records, made by the Original Dixieland Jazz Band in 1917. They toured England successfully throughout 1919, at the same time that the Southern Syncopators, featuring Sidney Bechet, were appearing in Paris, where Joyce would shortly compose "Circe." If he didn't know jazz, he certainly was familiar with ragtime. Irving Berlin's "Alexander's Ragtime Band" had been an international hit in 1911—Vernon and Irene Castle had danced the grizzly-bear to it in Paris, inspiring Severini (fig. 23)—and ragtime was being played throughout Europe. Eliot lamented this in *The Waste Land.* Joyce's cascading catalogs of names and quicksilver pub patter often do seem to be booted along and buoyed by the beat of some distantly heard music-hall rag, though he curiously fails to play this up, literally, on the pianola (mechanical

piano) in Bella Cohen's brothel, locus of the wildest behavior in
"Circe." In *James Joyce and the Making of "Ulysses"* (1934), Frank Bud-
gen, its author, a good friend of Joyce's, recalls how their conversation
in a Paris café was interrupted by the fierce pounding of a garishly lit
electric piano. " 'Look!' said Joyce. 'That's Bella Cohen's pianola. What
a fantastic effect! All the keys moving and nobody playing.' " His
excitement notwithstanding, the pianola is a negligible presence in
"Circe," blandly emitting five snatches of lyrics from the popular song
"My Girl's a Yorkshire Girl" (pages 575–78). The glittering, animated
pianola sounds oddly incoherent, to no effect—*"Bang fresh barang bang
of lacquey's bell, horse, nag, steer"*—where it might have served Joyce at
several junctures as a visually fantastic but credible source of Expressionist lighting and verbal music of a Kurt Weill kind (page 579). Professor Nabokov, who criticized Joyce's "needless obscurities," would
show Joyce the light in *Lolita* with one exact image of "those luminous
globules of gonadal glow that travel up the opalescent sides of juke
boxes" (a circa 1946 Wurlitzer).

The jazz-Joyce conjunction should be commemorated by an artist
commissioned to assemble a vernacular construct that would deceptively recall such Marcel Duchamp anti-art "ready-mades" as his *Bicycle
Wheel* of 1913, a metal wheel mounted on a painted wood stool. ("A
midget in a kindergarten," Saul Steinberg called Duchamp.) Our proposed exhibit—an evocation of aleatory jazz—would feature three rubber plungers and two water glasses painted blue (Jack Teagarden)
mounted on a worn wooden dance-hall floor and titled *The Brass Section.*
Installed in the Surrealism and Dada gallery on the second floor of the
Museum of Modern Art, along with famous assemblages of quirky or
throwaway stuff by Duchamp, Joseph Cornell, Meret Oppenheim, and
Man Ray, it would be the only irony-free, meaning-filled, unambiguous tribute in the gallery. (Man Ray's *Gift* [1921], typical of the
gallery—a painted flatiron with tacks on the bottom—may be a joke
about quixotic, self-canceling vanity or have no "meaning" at all.) Of
course, the meaning of *The Brass Section* would be almost as obscure as
"Oxen of the Sun" unless appropriate plunger-mute jazz was piped into
the gallery, culminating in Ellington's aleatory wonder, "Happy-Go-
Lucky Local" (1946), where the brass bears the heaviest load in simulat-
ing the sounds of a train that doesn't skip any junction stop, the
high-note trumpeter Cat Anderson effecting a long, screeching, brak-
ing, "phallocentric" halt. The last characterization has actually been
made. Some gallery-goers are swaying in place, recognizing for the first

110. Meret Oppenheim, *Object,* also known as *Luncheon in Fur,* 1936. Fur-covered cup, saucer, and spoon.

time the vaginocentric symbolism of Oppenheim's nearby *Luncheon in Fur* (1936), the cultural apotheosis of raw vernacular expression and a possibly comprehensible work, Armstrong's "Lazy River" scat in concrete form and insinuating words (fig. 110). "What could the spoon stand for?" asks a gallery-goer.

Problematic assemblages aside, the brass of Ellington and Teagarden is of course accessible and even *Ulysses* is not beyond rescue, especially if the reader isn't demoralized by "Proteus," the book's thorny third chapter, and simply skips the "Oxen of the Sun" section, as Professor Nabokov instructed his Cornell students to do, pausing only long enough to have them enter the specific names of seventeen parodied writers and genres ("Gothic novel") along the page margins of *Ulysses* "to illuminate your summer study of the novel," he said slowly, with a straight face, staring at the back of the room, fraternity row. *Lectures on "Ulysses"* (1980), a limited-edition facsimile of Nabokov's lecture notes, written in his own hand, is the prosecution's last and trump exhibit in the case against modernist obscurantism. The sole page devoted to "Oxen of the Sun" turns out to be in the hand of Véra, Nabokov's wife and assistant. Her list of the chapter's parodies is copied verbatim from Richard M. Kain's *Fabulous Voyager: James Joyce's "Ulysses"* (1947), and she cites her source cryptically at the top of the manuscript page. Evidently, master allusionist Nabokov hadn't recognized the parodies any better than legions of undergraduates. The state rests its case. The defense team is ashen, stunned speechless.

"Rhythm saved the world," sings Armstrong, and Joyce is readily comprehensible when he's got rhythm, as he does in the sociopolitical parodies of "Cyclops," comic invention and patter of "Circe," and rolling lyricism of "Penelope," the Molly Bloom chapter. Even if Mr. and Mrs. Bloom have no conjugal future, the entire chapter can move and inspire ordinary readers because it's the century's greatest piece of vernacular prose, its accessibility saved for the end because Joyce imagines his tidal, open-ended last chapter streaming into and rejuvenating the reader's world. It would be even more accessible on its own, set apart from the intimidating whole and published separately in a paperback titled *Blooming Molly,* say, with a questionable if not vulgar subtitle to attract the sexual self-help market or simply the shy and the glum, such as Fats Waller's immobilized dance pupil (fig. 20) or Matisse's deathly pale *The Italian Woman* (1916), who is disappearing into or behind the painting's self-reflexive, threatening curtain of malaise and imminent oblivion—World War I, no doubt, TOT by Carrà (fig. 98), anxiety everywhere, registered here by her cinematic stop motion or time-lapse jittery hands and the way the horror-film curtain is claiming her mourning-band black hair despite the dynamic character of her schematic, African-mask–like features, subliminal evidence of "primitive" strength (fig. 111).

The mourning bands are much larger in Matisse's *Goldfish and Palette* and *French Window at Collioure,* painted in 1914 immediately after the outbreak of war, the "palette" of the first title calling attention to the artist's mood and Matisse himself, seated just off-canvas on the right. His two tense, dark legs support the rectangular palette, his protruding thumb as deathly white as the color-free palette. Its coarse, heavily painted surface has been scratched and distressed, which calls attention to the tactile space and emphasizes the drama of its drained palette and the dangerously clouded condition of the fish water, since color is consciousness. The evolving blackness of the three pictures represents an eclipse, a crisis of self and society (figs. 111, 112, 113). No nocturnal sky is as unnaturally black as the view from *French Window at Collioure,* Matisse's own Riviera apartment; the strips of black on the left and in the foreground also render Matisse's figurative war-torn interior. (The blue and green are shutters, expressively pale.) Matisse's apartments usually overlooked the Mediterranean, as in his glimmering *Open Window, Collioure* (1905), which introduces his career-long open-window theme—the logical, vernacular emblem for perception and state of mind (for 1947, fig. 82). The structural (and subliminal?) Christian cross in the top right corner of *Goldfish and Palette* quietly signals that the painter, who in 1951 would austerely decorate the Chapel of the Rosary at Vence, is praying that more light and color will soon fill him.

In this context, *Violinist at the Window* (spring 1918) can be said to show Matisse parting the Black Sea (fig. 114). The arbitrary, quite unusual brown of the sky, which matches the violin and floor, is a harbinger of richer harmonies to come. Matisse, creator of *Interior with a Violin Case* (fig. 3), did play the violin, and his *Violinist at the Window* could serve as a frontispiece to the new edition, *Blooming Molly:* Joyce and the two Blooms battling their collective dolors, truly fiddling away the blues. The not altogether black and blues of Matisse's *The Silence Living in Houses* (1947) yearn to hear the green outside the closed window, an invalid's wish; Matisse's *Jazz,* his great escape, would soon appear (fig. 115). "O Jamesy let me up out of this," Molly directly addresses her maker when she menstruates unexpectedly in her bed in

III. Henri Matisse, *The Italian Woman*, 1916.

112. Henri Matisse, *Goldfish and Palette,* Autumn 1914.

113. Henri Matisse, *French Window at Collioure,* Autumn 1914.

114. Henri Matisse, *Violinist at the Window*, Spring 1918.

115. Henri Matisse, *The Silence Living in Houses*, 1947.

116. Artist unknown, *Turned-off Palette at High Noon.* In truth, a coffeehouse logo, France, 1933.

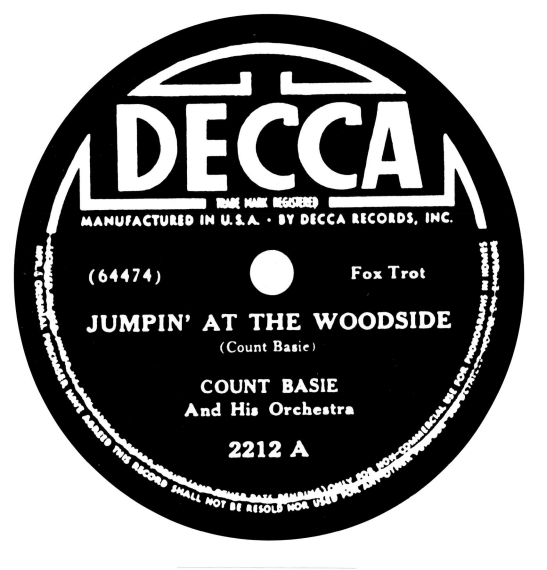

DECCA

TRADE MARK REGISTERED
MANUFACTURED IN U.S.A. · BY DECCA RECORDS, INC.

(64474)   Fox Trot

JUMPIN' AT THE WOODSIDE
(Count Basie)

COUNT BASIE
And His Orchestra

2212 A

117. 1938. Original label in blue.

the deep night (*Ulysses,* page 769). Music *is* transformative, but Matisse's palette is still stricken and stifled in *Violinist at the Window,* the player's stark cranium calling for a helmet or protective padding. The bottom half of this sea-view from Collioure or beachfront Nice—note the thin black horizon line—should in truth register some shade of Mediterranean blue instead of its sickly faint pink pallor, the White Sea deadness that reflects the heavy bank of (war?) clouds.

As with Armstrong, Matisse's high chromatic joys—often taken for granted or rejected as *his* rictus grin—become more compelling in the face of black chords and clouds such as these. *The Rumanian Blouse,* you remember, was completed by Matisse as the German army overran France in 1940 (fig. 75). As the cover illustration for *Blooming Molly, The Rumanian Blouse* should counteract but not compromise the requisite vulgarity of the enticing subtitle. Scholarly endnotes in the special edition would elucidate Molly's references to earlier events and characters. The introduction should seek to prepare the reader to negotiate the unpunctuated, rhythmic flow of Molly's uninhibited, knowledge-free, limited-vocabulary "deepdown torrent," Matisse by the Mediterranean at cloud-free high noon in July without sunglasses. "Mercy! Turn down that pal-ette!" dance instructor Waller might have shouted over the music.

The pulse of Molly's thoughts and reveries could be called jazzlike, the idea and potential of "Circe" 's pianola fully realized by Molly's Jolls-Joyce motor, the musical apotheosis of *Ulysses.* Her pulse is in fact logaoedic, a prose-poetic metrical rhythm first identified by the imperial Romans. "It Don't Mean a Thing (If It Ain't Got That Swing)," as Ivie Anderson sings with Ellington (1932), poor grammar a promise of uninhibited behavior. More precisely, the logaoedic is marked by a mixture of several exact meters—both dactyls and trochees or anapests and iambs—but follows no strict scansion. In jazz terms, Molly's pulse is at least fifteen years ahead of its time, more akin to Ellington's beat (he'd snap his fingers three times to set the tempo) and Basie's clockwork foursome of 1936–43—Jo Jones; Walter Page, bass; Freddie Green, guitar—than any clunky 1922 rhythm section. Molly's "syncopations" become palpable if one punctuates with slashes the opening passage of *Blooming Molly,* formulating a textbook example of logaoedic swing, an aid to readers and lovers in recovery:

Yes / because he never did a thing like that before / as ask to get his breakfast in bed / with a couple of eggs / since the *City*

Arms hotel / when he used to be pretending to be laid up with a sick voice / doing his highness to make himself interesting to that old faggot Mrs Riordan / that he thought he had a great leg of and she never left us a farthing / all for masses for herself and her soul / greatest miser ever was / actually afraid to lay out 4d for her methylated spirit / telling me all her ailments she had / too much old chat in her about politics and earthquakes and the end of the world / let us have a bit of fun first / God help the world if all the women were her sort / down on bathing suits and lownecks / of course nobody wanted her to wear / I suppose she was pious because no man would look at her twice / I hope Ill never be like her / a wonder she didnt want us to cover our faces / but she was a welleducated woman certainly / and her gabby talk about Mr Riordan here and Mr Riordan there / I suppose he was glad to get shut of her / and her dog smelling my fur and always edging to get up under my petticoats / especially then

The dog is more of a man than Bloom, it seems, and Joyce has beaten Hemingway in the underpublicized competition for Best Syncopated Prose. The runners-up, after "The Killers," are "Powerhouse," Julio Cortázar's *Hopscotch* (1966), Zora Neale Hurston's *Mules and Men* (1935), and Albert Murray's *Train Whistle Guitar* (1974).

Except for the final page-and-a-third of *Blooming Molly,* where Joyce doubles the tempo (a bebop convention of the 1950s), her monologue throbs at about eighty-six beats per minute on the metronome, a physiologically unremarkable pulse as steady and reassuring as the cardiovascular power of Jimmie Blanton's bass ostinato at the center of the Ellington ensemble and the unwavering metallic chomp-chomping of Jo Jones's hi-hat cymbals behind the Basie big band. Streamlined sans-serif, the most popular modernist typeface, was used as Decca's logotype in the thirties, and it represents the Basie pulse perfectly and suits his label-mates Jimmie Lunceford and Bing Crosby, too (fig. 117). To get the reader in the right groove, *Blooming Molly* should be packaged with a compact disc of jazz performances set on or very close to Molly's metronomic beat, which would include "I Got Rhythm," by the Jo Jones Trio (1959); "Just You, Just Me," by Big Sid Catlett's Band (1946); "I'm In the Mood for Love," by the Erroll Garner Trio (1951); "Pagin' the Devil," by Lester Young with the Basie-led Kansas City Six (1938, Jones on drums); "Perdido," by Ellington's band (1942, composed by his Puerto Rican valve-trombonist, Juan Tizol, whose several pieces added Caribbean hues to the entity); and "The Peanut Vendor," by Louis Armstrong and His Sebastian Cotton Club Orchestra (1931). Imported to America by the celebrated Cuban bandleader Don Azpiazu, who featured it with the dancer Alicia Parla in 1931 at New York's Paramount Theater, "The Peanut Vendor" ("El Manisero") started a national rumba craze. Armstrong's version, rather than Dizzy Gillespie's "Manteca" (1947) or Parker with Machito, constitutes the beginning of Afro-Cuban jazz in America. Gillespie's tenor saxophonist Big Nick Nicholas quotes Rodgers and Hart's "Blue Moon" during his dramatic solo on "Manteca," amid the roiling, clattering Latin rhythms— an incongruous Tin Pan Alley flourish that nonetheless makes sense as the mark of yet another node in the expanding Pan-American musical universe. The quotation evokes a moon over Miami and Havana, too, to fold in an old song title, the way Parker and Joyce often did, though the latter would hope we'd also recognize it as a gnomic allusion to a current political war.

Multiculturalism of a Latin sort courses genetically through *Blooming Molly,* whose girlhood on the Mediterranean isle of Gibraltar naturally makes her more unselfconsciously sensual to Joyce than any Celt. "Sex," according to an old punning joke, told with a brogue, "is the lack of the Irish." Molly Bloom thinks she might arouse her impotent husband if she got "a nice pair of red slippers like those Turks with the fez used to sell [on Gibraltar] or yellow and a nice semitransparent morning gown" (page 780), a Casbah outfit à la Matisse's bare-breasted *Odalisque in Red Trousers* (1921) or *Odalisque with Gray Culottes* (1926–27), where, as often occurs in such Matisses, the decor is more sexually charged than the woman because the room's unlikely, ill-coordinated colors and mismatched or clashing patterns represent improvisations of a kind—the erotic inventiveness and abandon she'll soon realize with her bedmate (fig. 119). That will be a jammed session indeed, analogous to Gjon Mili's (fig. 118), each slice of decor as one intense instrumental "chorus," no room to coast. Jo Jones would like this Matisse wall better than the ones he wanted to swing or embellish in *Interior with a Violin Case* (fig. 3). If the decorative panels are seen as comic-book "thought balloons," then this firm-breasted Odalisque is contemplating more than new wallpaper. There are no visual rests in the pattern, or need or even space for a rim shot by Jo Jones.

Odalisques were in fact Moroccan prostitutes (note the tentlike drapes) and conspicuous in French art history as painted by Ingres and

Delacroix. Matisse has at once aestheticized, and, in current terminology, "objectified" them—*his* jungle style—though any sexism or racialism is benign by the standards of 1927; French women didn't get the vote until October 1945, after World War II. In any event, Matisse's ladylike Parisian and Riviera Odalisques often look quite foolish costumed like harem girls in sedate bourgeois parlors. They might well have served as posh magazine illustrations of the latest 1920s or 1930s Victoria's Secret exotica/primitivist line—popular items, naturally, in the heyday of colonialism and kept women. Ireland fell short in both areas, but the British colony Gibraltar proved global enough for Joyce, who completed *Ulysses* in Paris, in 1921, where popular magazines such as *L'Illustration* regularly featured pictorials on "exotic" sun-kissed lands and people and coffeehouses were typically named La Maison D'Haiti, Café Negrilla, and Café Vieux Nègre, attempts to evoke twenty-one French colonies and protectorates (1945 population: 67 million) rather than warm-stemmed Josephine Baker alone (fig. 116). The large Exposition Coloniale opened in Marseilles in 1922, the year that *Ulysses* was published in Paris. Real Africans were imported to stock the Exposition's imaginary jungles, to revise Marianne Moore's definition of poetry.

Joyce becomes almost didactic about race and primal geography on the penultimate page of *Ulysses,* doubling Molly's pulse as she remembers the harbor of Gibraltar "and the Spanish girls laughing in their shawls and their tall combs and the auctions in the morning the Greeks and the Jews and the Arabs and the devil knows who else . . . and those handsome Moors all in white and turbans like kings" and the reader may recall Matisse's Moroccan paintings of 1912–13, especially the

OVERLEAF: 118. Is there a backup drummer in the house? Gjon Mili photographed this jam session at his studio loft, New York, 1943, where Mondrian often danced. Count Basie is at the piano, close to some of his own musicians—Earle Warren, alto sax on the left, and Lester Young above him. Kansas Fields is the drummer. Jo Jones, standing behind clarinetist Mezz Mezzrow, is itching to sit in. Kaiser Marshall, another drummer, is seated next to Basie. Big Sid Catlett, next to Jones, is snapping his fingers on cloud eight or nine, where music and musical prose should send us. Photo: TimePix.

FOLLOWING OVERLEAF: 119. Henri Matisse, *Odalisque with Gray Culottes,* 1926–27.

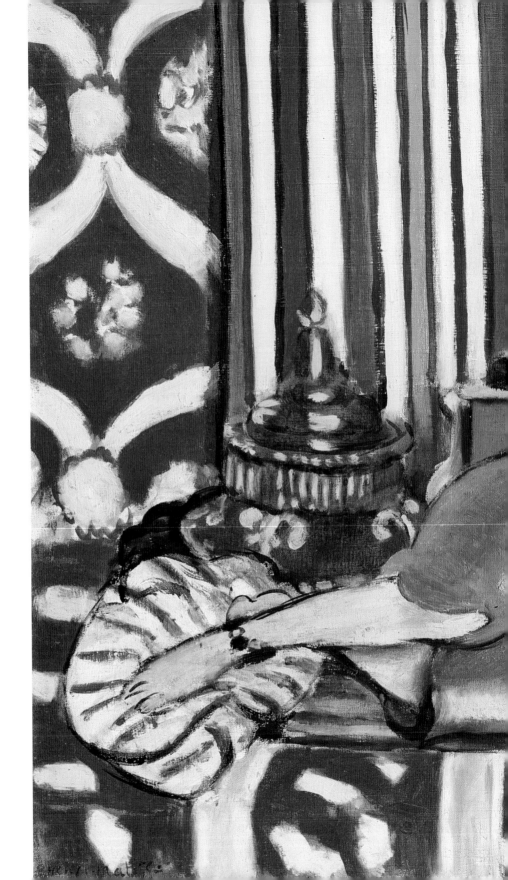

121. Henri Matisse, *Woman in Blue,* 1937.

brooding, brown-skinned, green-gowned Rif warriors and equally florid foliage and bursts of primary flowers that complement Joyce's prose here as it flows into the last page of *Ulysses,* where Molly the musing Odalisque remembers the sound of castanets and "O . . . the sea the sea crimson sometimes like fire and the glorious sunsets and the figtrees in the Alameda gardens yes and all the queer little streets and pink and blue and yellow houses and the rosegardens and the jessamine and geraniums and cactuses and Gibraltar as a girl where I was a Flower of the mountain yes when I put the rose in my hair like the Andalusian girls used or shall I wear a red yes" and then she remembers how she made love for the first time "under the Moorish wall," all of which brings Molly as close to sexy Africa as she'll ever get literally, like the *Odalisque with Gray Culottes* who only shares back-to-back space here with photographs of black players. The overt primitivism of the Molly passage, its open pantheism, Matisse palette, and musical prose constitute Joyce for everyone. The strategically placed Spanish castanets subliminally pepper and accentuate the pulse of the open-ended closing prose, along with whichever recommended record you're playing now and the close-up of sixty-five-year-old, hypertensive Armstrong holding nothing back. Isn't this what really embarrassed people about him?

"The Peanut Vendor," as it happens, is also grist for the jazz modernist's mill, a one-chord piece whose lyrics are too stupid for words. Armstrong only plays the theme once (muted), skips his customary vocal and trumpet variation and blissfully scats two choruses over a rumba beat, castanets clacking, calling out "Marie, Marie" from time to time, mysteriously ("my dear," "Cuba," "Spain" are comprehensible, isolated fragments), stretching and bending the two syllables of her name—"Ma-*ree,* Ma-*reeee!*" (vibrato on the second syllable)—as he swings lightly and loosely and carries us toward felicity. "Who is she, Pops?" asks a celestial Fats Waller, widening and rolling his eyes. "Brother Waller, and members of the congregation, that is my sister!"

OPPOSITE: 123. Matisse at work on a paper cutout at his Nice studio in 1952, two years before his death. Note *The Negress* (right rear), his monumental cutout in progress of 1953, an anachronistic throwback to Josephine Baker and the Cotton Club line—self-conscious, aestheticized primitivism's last Charleston or first rock-'n'-roll hop.

PRECEDING SPREAD: 122. Henri Matisse, *The Codomas,* from *Jazz,* 1947.

answers Armstrong, indignantly, and their laughter rocks the heavenly dance hall, where every figure and form is animated or dancing, as in the climactic Matisse, the truly swinging (it has two trapezes) self-projection of an ailing, often bedridden seventy-seven-year-old who would boogie like Mondrian (fig. 122). Armstrong scats another chorus, word-free, the castanets doubling their tempo. Even the squarest blacks are flying, as in the last Matisse, where they register a pulse as steady as Jo Jones's abiding hi-hats, which are chung-chunging off stage, 4/4 against the band's rumba beat, creating an uplifting rhythmic tension. Jones in fact played with Armstrong on one of his last TV appearances, February 1971 (he died in July), inspiring the stagnated All Stars and ailing trumpeter to play better than they had in some

124. Jean-Auguste-Dominique Ingres, *Portrait of Madame Ines Moitessier Seated,* 1856. Original in color.

time. The swelling black floor tiles of Matisse's *Woman in Blue* (1937) seem to have been dislodged by the seismic power of Armstrong's nearby trumpet (figs. 120, 121).

The *Woman in Blue* is Lydia Delectorskaya, Matisse's assistant, model, and possible mistress during the last two decades of his life. She often posed as an Odalisque, but there's no compromising hint of Morocco in *Woman in Blue*, a tribute to her character and role in Matisse's life. Its multiform point of view is radical, her frontal, symmetrical, frame-filling immense figure—it's only thirty-six inches high—recalling an iconic Russian church mosaic of a saint (Lydia was in fact Russian) set against the bifurcated, black tile floor "below." Part of Matisse is levitating above it, ecstatic—"riding on a C," in jazz parlance. Her face is repeated twice more in yellow and blue graven images that constitute a sustained chord—the operative word, along with *melody*. Most viewers will miss the icon template, and the way that Lydia's pose echoes Ingres's 1856 touchstone of refinement and poise, *Madame Ines Moitessier Seated*. These visual allusions are like the harmonic source of Charlie Parker's dozen or so compositions based on the chords of "I Got Rhythm"—likely to be spotted by musicians only (see page 48). Nor is the graphically ambiguous burst of yellow blossoms behind Lydia's head likely to be identified as a variation—or chordal change—on an Italian Old Master's most elaborate and grand gold-leaf aureoles, as in Piero della Francesca's *Madonna of Mercy* (after 1462) and Fra Angelico. But no one can miss the open melody of *Woman in Blue*, the floral spectacle as a sunrise (song lyrics to follow)—vernacular symbolism sharing the art summit, a paragon of jazz modernism, Matisse's devotion to this woman as clear as the "Jingle Bells" quoted by Charlie Parker on his rendition of "White Christmas," Christmas Eve, New York City, 1948, the year of the Irving Berlin airlift, to lighten history with music again. Malevich's *Suprematism: Self-Portrait in Two Dimensions* (1915) completes the picture, black on high (fig. 125), equal to the black plus sign in Stuart Davis's *Standard Brand* and higher than jazz was able to lift his bright pad (fig. 15)—"Black Beauty" most literally, chroma where it isn't supposed to exist. Doesn't this *Self-Portrait* look like felicity, peace of mind, and a balanced distribution of the humours (as the Elizabethans would say)? As with Mondrian, such high altitude should be grounded by live jazz.

Drummer Jones is smiling broadly from the wings, happy with the riffs and overall progression but a tad frustrated by his extended interactive role and absence from the spotlight. He looks eager to perform

125. Kasimir Malevich, *Suprematism: Self-Portrait in Two Dimensions*, 1915.

the tour de force he played almost nightly at the Embers in New York in the late 1950s with his own trio (piano and bass) on the old Count Basie–Harry Edison staple, "Jive at Five," using his hands on the snare drum instead of sticks or wire brushes. He'd announce the number by holding his hands up in the air, head-high, palms out to the audience, and, like a magician or a professor of surgery, he'd solemnly intone, "Five fingers on each hand," and flex his long digits. As the piano and bass played "Jive at Five," medium-tempo (like the Basie record), Jones's splayed hands would skate and swirl around the snare drum for several minutes, sounding like thick brushes, followed by his "drum solo"—a trick hands-and-fingers acoustic exercise to demonstrate that a simple snare drum has at least thirty distinct musical pitches, and Jones traveled up and down the scale, using one tamping hand to "tune" the taut calfskin, his facial tics and fleeting grimaces registering the intense, concentrated seriousness of his showmanship. Two fingertips concluded by performing a tapdance, a bit of jazz minimalism equivalent to Charlie Chaplin's *Gold Rush* dancing dinner rolls and Hemingway's victory with his plain but charged vocabulary in "The Killers," counted on five fingers: "Talk to me, bright boy." At a Newport jazz concert finale, circa 1967, consisting of unaccompanied solos by six or seven of the most technically brilliant drummers alive, the James Joyces of their instrument—including Elvin Jones, Mel Lewis, Louie Bellson, and Buddy Rich—Jo Jones, the oldest player, concluded the show alone on the stage equipped only with his hi-hat cymbal and a pair of sticks—no drums at all. "Papa Jo tore everybody apart," remembers Louie Bellson. "We all threw up our hands"—minimalist Hemingway outbeating Joyce, to pun simply, as Joyce sometimes does, agility and grit on the base paths instead of a home run. "Who could ask for a more efficacious denouement?" asks Professor Waller, pursing his lips and fluttering his eyelids.

OVERLEAF: 126. Pete Reiser of the Brooklyn Dodgers (right), still recovering from an almost fatal collision (see page 76), beats the tag by New York Yankees first baseman George McQuinn in the 1947 World Series. Photograph by Ernest Sisto / *The New York Times.*

THE END

List of Illustrations

New York. Photograph by David Heald Copyright © The Solomon R. Guggenheim Foundation, New York. Copyright © 2002 Artists Rights Society (ARS), New York/ADAGP, Paris.

Fig. 32: Constantin Brancusi, *King of Kings (Spirit of the Buddha),* c. 1938. Oak, 118⅜ × 19 × 18⅛″ (overall). Solomon R. Guggenheim Museum, New York. Photograph by David Heald Copyright © The Solomon R. Guggenheim Foundation, New York. Copyright © 2002 Artists Rights Society (ARS), New York/ADAGP, Paris.

Fig. 33: Pablo Picasso, *Nude with Raised Arms*, 1908. Gouache, 12⅝ × 9⅞″. Musée Picasso. Copyright © 2002 Estate of Pablo Picasso/Artists Rights Society (ARS), New York.

Fig. 34: Constantin Brancusi, *Danaïde*, 1913. Bronze with black patina and gold leaf, 10⅞ × 7⅛ × 8″ (overall, with limestone and oak base, 49″). Musée National d'Art Moderne, Centre Georges Pompidou, Paris. Copyright © 2002 Artists Rights Society (ARS), New York/ADAGP, Paris.

Fig. 35: Ben Shahn, *Welders*, 1943. Tempera on cardboard mounted on composition board, 22 × 39¾″. The Museum of Modern Art, New York. Copyright © 2001 The Museum of Modern Art, New York. Copyright © Estate of Ben Shahn/Licensed by VAGA, New York, N.Y.

Fig. 36: William P. Gottlieb, photograph of Charlie Parker and Red Rodney, New York, 1948. Copyright © William P. Gottlieb from the Library of Congress Collection.

Fig. 37: Henri Matisse, *Monsieur Loyal*, plate III from *Jazz*, 1947. Color stencil in gouache. National Gallery of Art, Washington. Gift of Mr. and Mrs. Andrew S. Keck. Photograph Copyright © 2001 Board of Trustees, National Gallery of Art, Washington. Copyright © 2002 Succession H. Matisse, Paris/Artists Rights Society (ARS), New York.

Fig. 38: A. M. Cassandre, *Pathé Electrique*, 1932. Poster. 15¾ × 23⅝″. Collection of the author.

Fig. 39: Piet Mondrian, *Composition with Red*, 1939. Oil on canvas, mounted on wood support. Wood support: 43 × 41¾ × 1″; canvas, $41\frac{7}{16} \times 40\frac{5}{16}$″. The Solomon R. Guggenheim Foundation, New York, Peggy Guggenheim Collection, Venice, 1976. Photograph by David Heald Copyright © The Solomon R. Guggenheim Foundation, New York. Copyright © 2002 Mondrian/Holzman Trust, c/o Beeldrecht/Artists Rights Society (ARS), New York.

Fig. 40: Piet Mondrian, *New York City I*, 1942. Oil on canvas, 46⅞ × 44⅞″. Musée National l'Art Moderne, Centre Georges Pompidou, Paris. Copyright © 2002 Mondrian/Holzman Trust, c/o Beeldrecht/Artist Rights Society (ARS), New York.

Fig. 41: Piet Mondrian, *Broadway Boogie Woogie*, 1942–43. Oil on canvas, 50 × 50″. The Museum of Modern Art, New York. Purchase. Photograph Copyright © 2001 The Museum of Modern Art, New York. Copyright © 2002 Mondrian/Holzman Trust, c/o Beeldrecht/Artist Rights Society (ARS), New York.

Fig. 42: Piet Mondrian, *Victory Boogie Woogie*, 1942–44. Oil and paper on canvas, 70¼″ diagonal. Private Collection. Copyright © 2002 Mondrian/Holzman Trust, c/o Beeldrecht/Artist Rights Society (ARS), New York.

Fig. 43: Artist unknown, "Victory Red" lipstick ad, c. 1942–43. Collection Karen Oshman.

Fig. 44: Photographer unknown, the 1941 Brooklyn Dodgers's infield. Collection of the author.

Fig. 45: Henry Koerner, poster for the U.S. Office of War Information, 1943. 28½ × 40″. Collection of the author.

Fig. 117: 1938 Decca record label. Collection of the author.

Fig. 118: Gjon Mili, jam session at his studio, featuring Count Basie, New York, 1943. Courtesy TimePix.

Fig. 119: Henri Matisse, *Odalisque with Gray Culottes*, 1926–27. Oil on canvas, 21¼ × 25½″. Musée de l'Orangerie, Paris. Collection Walter-Guillaume. Copyright © 2002 Succession H. Matisse, Paris/Artists Rights Society (ARS), New York.

Fig. 120: Philippe Halsman, *Louis Armstrong*, 1966. Copyright © Halsman Estate.

Fig. 121: Henri Matisse, *Woman in Blue*, 1937. Oil on canvas, 36½ × 29″. Philadelphia Museum of Art. Gift of Mrs. John Wintersteen. Copyright © 2002 Succession H. Matisse, Paris/Artists Rights Society (ARS), New York.

Fig. 122: Henri Matisse, *The Codomas*, plate XI from *Jazz*, 1947. Color stencil in gouache. National Gallery of Art, Washington. Gift of Mr. and Mrs. Andrew S. Keck. Photograph Copyright © 2001 Board of Trustees, National Gallery of Art, Washington. Copyright © 2002 Succession H. Matisse, Paris/Artists Rights Society (ARS), New York.

Fig. 123: Hélène Adant, photograph of Matisse at work in his Nice studio, 1952. Musée National d'Art Moderne, Centre Georges Pompidou, Paris.

Fig. 124: Jean-Auguste-Dominique Ingres, *Portrait of Madame Ines Moitessier Seated*, 1856. Oil on canvas, 47¼ × 36¼″. The National Gallery, London.

Fig. 125: Kasimir Malevich, *Suprematism: Self-Portrait in Two Dimensions*, 1915. Oil on canvas, 31½ × 24⅜″. Stedelijk Museum, Amsterdam.

Fig. 126: Pete Reiser of the Brooklyn Dodgers beats the tag by George McQuinn, 1947 World Series. Photograph by Ernest Sisto/*The New York Times*. Copyright © 2002 The New York Times Company.

Fig. 127: 1935 Decca record label. The second side of this Armstrong disk bears "Red Sails in the Sunset." Collection of the author.

Index

A NOTE ON THE TYPE

The text of this book was set in Garamond No. 3. It is not a true copy of any of the designs of Claude Garamond (c. 1480–1561), but an adaptation of his types, which set the European standard for two centuries. It probably owes as much to the designs of Jean Jannon, a Protestant printer working in Sedan in the early seventeenth century, who had worked with Garamond's romans earlier, in Paris, but who was denied their use because of Catholic censorship. Jannon's matrices came into the possession of the Imprimerie nationale, where they were thought to be by Garamond himself, and were so described when the Imprimerie revived the type in 1900. This particular version is based on an adaptation by Morris Fuller Benton.

Composition and color separations by
North Market Street Graphics, Lancaster, Pennsylvania

Printed and bound by Quebecor Cayfosa, Barcelona

Designed by Iris Weinstein